Duvall Football

— Winning a National Championship

Harold (Deacon) Duvall

Coach Harold "Deacon" Duvall

Duvall Football
— Winning a National Championship

Harold (Deacon) Duvall

NAIA Football Hall of Fame
West Virginia Football Hall of Fame
NAIA 1967 National Coach of the Year

Edited by Stephen Lipscomb

Copying and reprinting:

Library of Congress Cataloging-in-Publication Data: 2008903203
Author, Duvall, Harold, 1917–
Editor, Lipscomb, Stephen, 1944–
Title, Duvall Football — Winning a National Championship
ISBN 0-87012-744-8

Cover Design: For their help with designing the cover of this book, the author and editor give thanks to Adam Zundell at Fairmont State University, and, Gabriel Rubalcava, owner of the Fredericksburg Press.

Publication: In April of 2008 McClain Printing Company agreed to produce the first printing of (the first edition of) Duvall Football — Winning a National Championship. Only 500 perfect-bound books were printed, and this book is one of those 500. For their contributions supporting the publication of this book, the author and editor give thanks to Kenny Miller and Gary Moyer.

McClain Printing Company
Parsons, West Virginia
www.mcclainprinting.com
2008

Dedicated to

All of the fine young men whom
I have had the privilege to coach

and

The memory of
my wife Florence and our daughter Lynn

and

My wife Joan and my daughter Susan

Contents

Acknowledgments

The backbone of worthwhile accomplishments is mostly substantial effort and hard work. And in addition to substantial effort and hard work, specialized knowledge and technology may also be required.

In particular, in 1952 when I started my college-coaching career typewriters were at the forefront of technology. And during my two decades (1952–1972) as a college coach, I had no secretary.

For the first 15 of those years, I had my wife's help and I am still grateful. But then I needed a Play Book for each of my players, and I had access to neither the specialized knowledge nor the technology required to produce such books.

At that time, however, a relatively-new receptionist, a receptionist who had an exceptional gift for typing and organizing — the best I have ever witnessed — volunteered to produce the Play Book. She even created a Christmas letter for the parents of each team member that contained a Santa, his Reindeer, and a sack full of team victories. Her name is Nancy White — she could type full speed while she simultaneously talked on the phone and carried on a conversation with a student. She never stopped asking, *When are you going to write your book?*

Nancy also encouraged me to focus on my book by agreeing to type the initial posting — she would have completed the first draft had her health not intervened. So for her substantial contribution I thank and acknowledge Nancy from the bottom of my heart — and wish her good health.

After my own health concerns led me to question my ability to finish my book, the Good Lord sent one of my former players — a fine athlete, a distinguished mathematician, and a man I am proud to call Dr. Stephen Lipscomb — who volunteered to edit my book. I feel privileged to have had his help. All of what is important and most difficult is the work of this fine gentleman.

And finally, to his wife Patty, who proof read, corrected, and gave us a different perspective, I cannot thank her enough.

Locations of WVIAC Schools of Interest

Formed in 1924 with 14 Charter Members, the *West Virginia Intercollegiate Athletic Conference* "WVIAC" has been mostly comprised of various West Virginia Colleges and Universities.[1]

The locations illustrated below concern the colleges and universities that are most relevant to the stories in this book.

[1]The Charter Members of concern in this book are Concord, Davis & Elkins, Fairmont State, Glenville State, Salem, West Liberty State, West Virginia Tech, West Virginia University, and West Virginia Wesleyan. Over the years, however, the WVIAC membership has been fluid: Some schools have left the conference and have not returned, e.g., West Virginia University left in 1927; others have left the conference only to return at a later date; new members schools, some from outside of West Virginia, have joined the conference; and others have replaced the "college" part of their name, with "university." Currently, the WVIAC has 16 members.

Editor's Introduction

WHAT ARE THE ODDS? Prior to 1967, the odds that a Division II West Virginia College would win a *national* football championship were immeasurably small.

Why? One reason was that these Colleges had *no* football scholarships, while some of their national-champion competitors had almost 50.

And what reduced the odds further was West Virginia's relatively-small population, which translates to relatively few "blue-chip" (exceptional) players. For example, because of the 1970 disparity of populations between West Virginia and Michigan, it is reasonable to estimate that for each football player in West Virginia, Michigan had five.[1]

1940 Populations

U.S.	131 million
Michigan	5.3 million
W.Va.	1.9 million
Fairmont	23 thousand

1970 Populations

U.S.	200.3 million
Michigan	8.9 million
W.Va.	1.74 million
Fairmont	26 thousand

The odds prior to 1967 become even smaller when you consider that *no* West Virginia School had ever won a national football championship! And the odds prior to 1967 become yet again smaller because Bobby Bowden, who currently holds the record for the most victories in NCAA Division I football and who has won a national championship, did not win a national championship while coaching in West Virginia. Recall the ending to that famous cheer? ... Bobby Bobby he's our man, if he can't do it (in West Virginia), then no-body can. It is against this backdrop that *Harold Deacon Duvall defies all odds by coaching the first team from West Virginia to win a national football championship.*[2]

Starting with Chapter 1 below, Coach Duvall tells us his unbelievable (David verses Goliath) story — his values, his struggles on and off the field, and his view of building a championship football team. Looking back, the sentiments imbedded in Ronald Reagan's view that *America is too great to dream small* describe Coach Duvall's accomplishment — *When it comes to coaching football, Deacon Duvall was too great to dream small.*

[1]For the 1940 data, see The American Educator Encyclopedia (1943), and for the 1970 data, see the Encyclopædia Britannica (1974).

[2]The team is the 1967 Fairmont State team: Founded in 1865 as West Virginia Normal School at Fairmont, West Virginia, Fairmont State was dedicated to educating teachers. It was purchased by the State and became Fairmont State Normal School in 1867. It was renamed Fairmont State Teachers College in 1931, and Fairmont State College in 1943. In 2004, the state allowed Fairmont State College to change its name to Fairmont State University. Currently, enrollment is about 8,000, and Fairmont State's athletic teams, known as the Falcons, compete in the West Virginia Intercollegiate Athletic Conference (WVIAC) in NCAA Division II.

But let us not get ahead of ourselves. To appreciate such an exceptional feat, we start at the beginning. (The circumstances that nurtured such an accomplishment are presented at the end of book in the Editor's Postscript.)

Nature Takes its Course

In 1917, following repeated attacks by German U-boats on neutral shipping, the United States entered World War I. In joyful contrast, it was January 11, 1917 that 28 year-old Bessie Duvall and her 32 year-old husband, Frank Duvall, gave birth to their first child — Harold.[3]

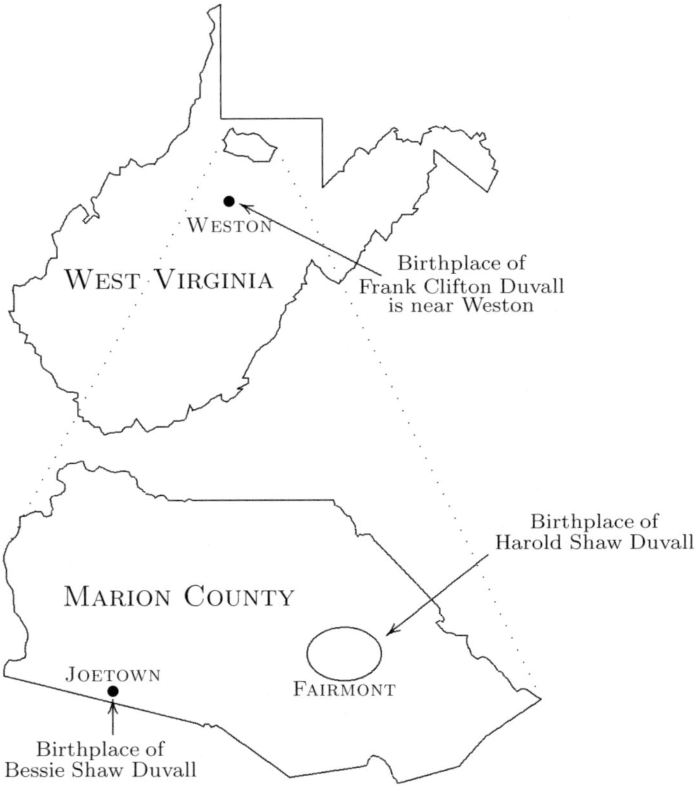

The Nickname "Deacon"

"Harold Duvall" is today widely known as "Coach Duvall," or, "Deacon Duvall," or, most simply, either "Deacon" or "Coach." It was his father Frank who was first known as "Deacon," and it was one of Frank's friends who first called Harold, who was a young boy at the time, "Little Deacon."

[3]Harold Shaw Duvall was born in Fairmont, West Virginia; and more than eight years would pass before Bessie Lenore (Shaw) Duvall (September 1888 – August 1982) and Frank Clifton Duvall (October 1884 – April 1962) had their second and last child, Edith May (Duvall) Jefferson. Among world events, World War I dates from 1914 to 1918.

CHAPTER 1

First Year as College Coach
Part I: First Four Days

It was April 1952. The Fairmont State Athletic Director, Jasper Colebank, was retiring, and the head basketball coach, Wilford (Squibb) Wilson, was in line to become the next Athletic Director. So for the 1952-53 school year, Fairmont State would need a new head coach for basketball.

I had known Squibb since 1935, when he was a senior and I was a freshman at Fairmont State. But in 1952, I was coaching at a local high school, and, for whatever reasons, Squibb inquired about my interest in the position of Head Basketball Coach at Fairmont State. I told him that I was very interested.

Outside of athletics, however, the administration was facing other "adjustments." In particular, one of the professors told her art class that she was an agnostic. At that time, West Virginia had some southern roots resembling the Bible belt.

In the 1950s such statements to students were of concern to many; and one member of the State Board of Education challenged the Professor, which eventually led to the Professor's dismissal.

Of course this sensitive situation aroused a huge public debate and even received national attention. And because the President of Fairmont State, Henry Hand, took the position of defending his faculty member, his time and concerns for athletics necessarily suffered. Nevertheless, three months after I had talked with Squibb about coaching basketball, the President and I scheduled an interview.

But on the day of the interview, the headline of the local newspaper stated that the President of Fairmont State was fired.

Two weeks later, I received a phone call from John Pence, one of my professors when I was a student at Fairmont State. John indicated that he would be replacing Henry Hand as President, and that he wanted to reschedule my interview. The interview was successful, and I was hired.

Basketball or Football?

Approximately one month prior to the start of the 1952 fall semester, I learned that I would not be the Head Basketball Coach, but instead, the Head Football Coach. Being the newest kid on the block, I felt that I had no choice but to agree. In those days there were no contracts, just handshakes.

The sudden change was, to say the least, a bit shocking — I was just starting my first year at Fairmont State, and in three weeks we would be on the football field. The change was justifiable, however, because the assignments were made in order to better serve the needs of the students.

In need of a Football Philosophy

To get up-to-speed as quickly as possible, I made a suggestion to Squibb, who had been the head football coach the past year and who was familiar with the abilities and football experience of the players. I suggested that he remain head coach for the upcoming football season, and that I would be his assistant. In addition, I would do all the legwork, e.g, assume various responsibilities such as equipment needs, and that he would only need to make the major decisions. Squibb did not agree. So I focused all of my attention on building a football program.

With the opening of fall practice only two weeks away, I pondered the question, *What system of offense should I use*? I reasoned that the best person to help me answer this question was the ex-coach.

Squibb's advice was that I should use the system that the players used the previous year; and he referred me to his quarterback, John Vernall. Evidently John was not only a player from the previous season, John had also helped Squibb install the offense. I also learned that John was returning for his senior year, and that he would soon be on campus.

I had mixed emotions about Squibb's advice because I had substantial experience and success with the "Notre Dame T." Indeed, under the "T" system over two seasons, the 1950 and 1951 seasons, my high-school team went ten wins, five losses, and one tie. And being the second smallest high school in a county of eight, we were mostly competing against larger schools.

So I was in a quandary — either use a football philosophy (the Notre Dame T) that I had already coached, or, use one that I had never coached.

Notre Dame T

The so-called "Notre Dame T" was developed by Frank Leahy. (Leahy published his book *Notre Dame Football — the* T *formation* in 1949.) The philosophy behind the T formation is that of having the quarterback do a *reverse pivot*, i.e, spin around (180°) so his back was to the line of scrimmage. This pivot would hopefully freeze the defensive linemen just long enough to slow their charge, making it easier for our offensive linemen to block. Coach Leahy reasoned that when the defense lost sight of the ball, they would hesitate until they located the ball.

The life span for the Notre Dame T included the late 1940s and early 1950s when the concept was new; and coaches had not had time to study the new philosophy. As a result, the Notre Dame T was highly successful.

It is difficult to estimate how long it takes for defenses to adapt to a new scheme. But all systems have their strengths and weaknesses; and given time, a good defensive coach will remove the element of surprise and then devise a scheme to counter the new system.

Even today, the key is surprise. With modern technology, defensive and offensive coaches can make adjustments almost from one series of plays to the next. In the 1950s, however, Fairmont State had no telephone system, no video tape, no pictures of every play an opponent ran in the latest series of downs, and none of the many other devices that are used to keep a coach instantly updated on the "most recent move" of the opponent.[1]

While the T-formation scheme was an option, I had experience with other systems and I needed time to reflect on which system would be the best for a team playing in the WVIAC.

Other Systems of Offense

When I coached in high school, we used the *single wing* and the *buck-lateral* systems. And as a football player (1935–1939) at Fairmont State, I had experienced the *single wing* and *double wing*.

The double wing in the 1930s–40s was a version of an offense that is now called the *shotgun* — prior to the snap, the quarterback is 3-to-6 yards behind the center. As employed during the late 1930s, however, my experience with the shotgun scheme left me with the belief that it was an unsophisticated offense.

For an example of my negative experience with the shotgun system, I recall playing in the system as the *motion man*. That is, on each play I would move (prior to the snap) from the left to the right side of the formation until I was positioned five yards outside my right end. To avoid the backfield-in-motion penalty, I always had to be careful not to turn up field prior to the snap. Once I turned up field, I would try to sprint past the defensive halfback. We always ran the motion from the left to the right side, and I was the only motion man. Since the motion was repeated on every play, it served no purpose because it was not confusing the defense. I realized the futility of exerting so much energy in a scheme that did nothing to improve our chances of winning.

Systems of offense ranging from the "single wing" to the "T-formation" were options for the Fairmont State team. But I did not want to put the "cart before the horse." That is, I had neither any idea about the talents of the Fairmont State players nor the system that these players had experienced in

[1]Furthermore, Fairmont State did not provide an assistant coach. On the positive side, however, most of the other coaches in the conference were working under similar conditions — as I now recall, only two of 12 colleges in our league had an assistant.

prior years; and to have success, a coach must first know the players' talents and players' experience so that he can then select a matching offense.

Nevertheless, my state of mind at the time made me somewhat secure because I had always studied systems of offense; I felt that I was mostly up-to-date; and I had convinced myself that I had knowledge, even if somewhat limited, of most of the known systems of the time.

If there were an exception to the schemes of offense that I knew, it was the system know as the *Split*-T. In short, I knew almost nothing about Split-T football. But first things first, I was very anxious to speak with John Vernall, the returning senior quarterback, to learn about the players and the system of offense used in the previous year.

When John arrived on campus, and we finally met, I inquired about the system of offense that was employed during the previous year. He immediately replied that it was the "Split-T." I was totally shocked! His answer told me that what I knew and what my players knew about offense could not have been further apart.

And there were other considerations. In particular, for my first season at Fairmont State I would have 25 players, and nine of the 25 were returning. I was sitting on the two horns of a dilemma — if I used the Split-T, then the learning burden would fall on me and the 16 new players; but if I didn't use the Split-T, then the burden would fall on all 25 players.

So I had a problem that needed an immediate solution. I faced such situations as a young boy growing up on a farm where I learned early on that I had to solve problems head on. I could make no excuses — you immediately take care of your farm animals, or you will be out of the farming business.

The Split-T

In 1943 Bud Wilkinson joined the U.S. Navy and served as an assistant to Don Faurot with the Iowa Pre-Flight Seahawks football team. Faurot is credited with inventing the Split-T formation.[2]

The best way to contrast the "Split-T" with the "Notre Dame T" is to simply state that the rationale used to justify the Split-T scheme was completely opposite to the rationale used to justify the Notre Dame T.

The Split-T was founded on the idea of spreading the defense so as to create "natural seams or holes" where the backs on offense could run through before the defense could adjust. Wilkinson's Split-T offense would line up

[2]In 1946, following World War II, Jim Tatum persuaded Wilkinson to join his staff at Oklahoma. Then Tatum goes to Maryland, and Wilkinson becomes head coach. At Oklahoma (1947–63) Wilkinson's teams set the NCAA Division I consecutive-games-won record at 47-straight. The streak, spanning five seasons 1953-57, is considered one of the greatest feats in major college football history. Wilkinson also led Oklahoma on a 31-game winning streak from 1948-50.

at the line of scrimmage so that the distance between adjacent linemen was 1–to–1$\frac{1}{2}$ yards. To compensate, the defense would then line up with similar spacing between adjacent linemen, which would spread the defense. Further, the offensive backs would line up only about 2–to–2$\frac{1}{2}$ yards behind the tackles and "run to daylight" before the defense could react.

To decrease defense-reaction time even further, the quarterback would move directly down the line of scrimmage, as opposed to the reverse pivot which requires time for the the quarterback to pivot. The logic was to get the ball to the running back at the line-of-scrimmage as soon as possible.

Today, many coaches believe that a good offense is one that provides players with the *option to adapt as a play develops* — on option plays the quarterback has the option of keeping the ball or handing off. Also, as a play develops and a pass receiver finds himself being guarded on his outside shoulder, he may have the option to adjust his pass route to go inside and move away from the defender. With or without option plays, a coach must balance, or complement, his running game with a passing game because a "one-dimensional offense" gives his opponent's defense an advantage.

At the time when the Split-T was introduced, I was like many coaches who did not see its potential — I had neither the expertise nor the experience to realize that the sky was the limit when it comes to schemes for the offense.

The Split-T was flexible, i.e., coaches could devise their own system. But when it was new, coaches ran it like their forefathers, i.e., the hard way.

Preparing for the First Practice

It was Friday, and by Monday we would have our first practice. I had learned from John Vernall, our quarterback, that last-year the team had used the Split-T offense; and so I had decided that it would be best for the team to stay with what they already knew.[3]

To learn the subtleties of the Split-T offense, I studied the book *Oklahoma Split-*T by Bud Wilkinson. Because of Wilkinson's success with his offense, it was generally accepted that when someone used the phase "Split-T," they were referring to *Bud Wilkinson's system of offense.* It never occurred to me that there may be other books by other coaches with other variants of Wilkinson's Split-T.

In addition to learning a new offense, I had yet to learn how to properly prepare at the college level. In contrast, at the high-school level I had obtained acceptable results even when I wasn't properly prepared. Perhaps the boys at the high-school level in 1950s would simply put aside any observable

[3]For eight years at the high-school level I had used several systems, and over those last two years I saw real progress with one particular scheme. Unfortunately, that scheme wasn't the Split-T. In other words, rather than install a system that made me feel comfortable, I felt that it was best for the team to continue with the Split-T.

shortcomings in my preparation.

Also in retrospect, after three days of studying the Split-T, I was glad that I did not have to explain the system to an assistant.[4]

I read Wilkinson's Split-T book in its entirety, twice. Although the system was contrary to what I had taught in the past, I had a good feeling about the new system. I understood the reasons that justified the line splits, I understood the "calls" telling the halfback where to run, and I understood how to make the system productive.

By Sunday evening, I made a players notebook. It only had four pages, but it contained the basics of the system — I wanted everyone on the same page. My very good secretary, my wife, helped produce 20 copies. (In 1952, neither any faculty member nor the Department had a secretary.)

First Practice — Reverse Pivot?

At the beginning of practice, I handed the four-page notebook to the seven returning regulars. Since there were more than 20 candidates, and I had only 20 booklets, I randomly distributed the remaining notebooks, telling those who had a copy to share their copy with those who did not. Looking quizzingly at each other, the seven returnees studied their notebooks. But I sensed a feeling of uneasiness. Nothing was said, however, and so I started to step the players through the physical techniques that are required to execute the Spit-T.

Following Wilkinson's logic, the first priority at the first practice was to start the quarterback and center working on the exchange, i.e., the *snap*. After the exchange, the quarterback gets the ball as quickly as he can to the halfback by *stepping across*, which is *not a reverse pivot*. Because Wilkinson was so successful, I wanted to teach it exactly as he described it — without deviations.

At first, I felt like I was just not ready to teach. I was impatient to see the center make his first "snap." The center was the only player I knew before coming to Fairmont State (he had played in Marion county and I had seen him play several games in high school). He was a very good, reliable, and hard-nosed athlete; although he was small for a college player.

I am now ready to witness the center and quarterback exchange. To my extreme surprise, the center snaps the ball and the *quarterback does a reverse pivot*. I'm dumbfounded! *A reverse pivot in the Split*-T *system*? It can't be. According to Wilkinson's "football bible" that is not what the

[4]Pi Davis, the basketball coach, had been assistant football coach the previous year. In 1952 he was also the County Playground Director, and the date of closure was not until after the start of the fall semester. So Pi could not assist in football until the second or third week of football practice. It turned out that Pi coached the cross country team during the fall semester, leaving me with no assistants.

quarterback does in the Split-T.

Recalling that the quarterback, John Vernall, had already said that he had played quarterback in the Split-T system, I immediately told John that the quarterback does *not* do a reverse pivot in the Oklahoma Split-T — it was always a direct hand off. So I asked him, "Where did you learn the Split-T?" He said that he learned it from a book that he had in his room.

I asked John to go to his room and bring his book to the practice field. When he returned, he showed me the book *Football: Secrets of the "Split-T" Formation* by Don Faurot, which was published in 1950.

Don Faurot, who is he? He was a Football Coach at Missouri University, and sure enough his version of the Split-T shows a reverse pivot. And even worse, not one, but all plays begin with a reverse pivot. This system involves not only the quarterback faking and hiding the ball, but there are many counters, crosscuts, delays, and trap plays.[5]

Although the "*What is the Split-T?*" dilemma occurred over 50 years ago, I have yet to understand how those fine young men worked through the mess that I created on that first day. Simply put, I was frustrated, embarrassed, and obviously unprepared. At least I understood the baffled facial expressions of the seven regulars when they viewed my Split-T notebook.

First Four Days of Practice

Despite the breakdown in communication between the players and myself over the meaning of the Split-T, even more shocking events soon followed.

The first four days of practice were the four worst days of my athletic life. I can only surmise that a similar feeling spread throughout the squad, especially the seven returning regulars. We worked together, but there was an ambiance of uncertainty.

The quarterback was the coach; the seven regulars knew what was expected; and two talented freshmen filled a void created by graduation.

One of the freshmen was a high-school center and the other was a tackle. We inserted the high school tackle not into the tackle position, rather into the end position. We used the high-school center, who weighed 205 lbs and had good quickness, as a tackle. To back-up the freshman tackle, we used another good center.

In those days, the offensive players also played defense.

Injuries to players were always a concern, but we were fortunate that

[5] On the day of our first practice, I had never even heard of Don Faurot or Jim Tatum; and I did not know of the Bud Wilkinson, Don Faurot, and Jim Tatum connection (see first few paragraphs in "The Split-T" section and footnote 2 above where the "connection" is detailed). Evidently all three wrote books on the Split-T — each had his own philosophy, the three philosophies differed significantly, but each called their system the Split-T. Wilkinson's version of the Split-T, however, set the consecutive-wins record at 47.

almost all injuries were not serious.

By the end of the first four days, all positions on the first two units were nearly settled. There will always be some fine young man who will be overlooked, but if you are attentive, you will see the cream come to the top. Our quarterback and at least the seven veterans seemed to know what they were doing. In contrast, I was sure that I did not know what I was doing; and I was also sure that we were headed for disaster.

Then, the unthinkable happens.

Fourth Day, Three Players Lost

In the afternoon of the fourth day of practice, namely Thursday, I learned that our quarterback, John Vernall, our All-Conference offensive right tackle, John DePasquale, and our offensive left end, Frank Stingo, were reporting for induction into the Armed Forces. And yes, they were reporting the next day, Friday. More than position players, however, the quarterback and the All-Conference player were among three of the seven regulars who were, in effect, coaching the team.

Perhaps I was afraid to ask, but I will never know whether or not they had enlisted. Would they really prefer bullets over footballs?

Pressure Builds

From that first day of practice, when it became clear to the players that I was unaware of the variation of the Split-T known as the "Faurot Split-T," I felt pressure to prove myself to my players. And now, with our loss of three key players, the future for the team looked bleak. I knew I had to win a respectable number of games to have an acceptable season. But the pressure was not only coming from the need to win, but also from the fact that I had a one-year contract. In short, as the coach I had to take control.

Finding a Quarterback

A coach must not be distracted by events that are out of his control. We had just lost our starting quarterback, so we had to move on. *Who would be our quarterback?*

All I knew to do was ask the squad. Two players said that they had experience at the quarterback position. One was the left end from the previous year who had played some quarterback in the tenth grade. His name was Blaine Morton. The other was a candidate for a halfback position.

I made my first wise decision — I made both of them quarterbacks. I cannot yet understand why the good Lord smiled on me. Blaine was a super athlete who fit the Split-T to a "T." That is, he was athletic and an average passer — even though he did not throw neat spirals, his accuracy was average. In this Wilkinson Split-T, Blaine would only be required to throw a pass on rather rare occasions, and when he did pass, it would usually be either a jump pass or a short pass. It turned out that Blaine only needed 30+ passes for the whole season.

Selecting an Offense

It seemed like a déjà-vu moment. Again, I was trying to select the best offensive system. Should we adopt the Notre Dame T, the Faurot Split-T, or, the Wilkinson Split-T?

I had issued my little notebook on the Wilkinson's Split-T, we were practicing Faurot's Split-T, and I had had success with the Notre Dame T. The (Faurot) Missouri Split-T was similar to the Notre Dame T in that it begins with the reverse pivot, which required delicate footwork while faking with the ball and running trap plays.

My love of the trapping game grew out of my experience as a coach at a small high school where we constantly played larger schools with much larger players. Smaller boys can compete with the larger boys if they don't have to go head to head. My 130-pound boy couldn't be expected to manhandle a 170-pounder head on. If, however, the 130-pound blocker uses a *trap block*, a block from the side and not head on, he can neutralize the 170-pound tackler's size and charge. In fact, the chance of success of a trap block increases in direct proportion to the speed of the tackler's charge. These facts come out of the Notre Dame T. Yes, I wanted to use this system.

Nevertheless, my decision was to go with the Wilkinson Split-T. My reasoning was that my end-converted-to-quarterback had never taken a snap at the college level; the reverse pivot is very difficult to learn; and we had only eight days to get ready. The chances for success would increase if we used the Wilkinson Split-T, which was easy to learn in a short time.[6]

I had almost discarded my little four-page playbook, but I brought it back, hoping that the players had also saved their copies. Since classes would not begin until Monday and our first game was scheduled for the following Saturday, we could practice twice Friday and twice Saturday, and then once-per-day for the five days of the following week. Because I was once again leading the team, I was beginning once again to feel like a coach.

---

[6]When I started to train my high school quarterback for the reverse pivot, I did as Coach Leahy suggested — I started in the gym on a hard floor with gym shoes. I had three months to teach the pivots and the ball handling techniques. Comparing three months of training to only the eight days that were left prior to our first game, the reverse pivot was not the answer for this team.

CHAPTER 2

First Year as College Coach
Part II: Last Eight Days of Training

From Chapter 1, recall that I became Head Coach of Football at Fairmont State a few weeks prior to our 1952 season; while trying to learn Fairmont State's previous football system, I had let the quarterback be the coach for four days; mistakenly assuming that Fairmont's 1951 Split-T was the Oklahoma Split-T, I placed myself in an embarrassing situation; after just four days of practice and eight days before our first game, we lost our starting quarterback and two regulars; and, because we lost key players, I adopted the Oklahoma Split-T, an offensive system that I had never coached.

Installing the Wilkinson Split-T

On the afternoon of our fourth day of practice, we started installing the Oklahoma Split-T. It was no big deal — there were no sports writers, very few spectators, and not many fans. It was most likely that none of our faithful knew anything about the Split-T offense, which was a plus because there were a minimum of distractions. Indeed, we did not have outside people giving "free advice." The faithful didn't want to see the practices and we didn't want to explain what we were doing.

In three practice sessions, one on Thursday and two on Friday, we went over and over a few basic plays: The quickie (halfback hand off), the slant, the fullback off tackle, the option, the toss to the other halfback running wide, the quarterback keeper, and a jump pass. When installing a new offense, a coach needs to be careful about introducing too many plays too fast. It is far better to execute a few plays well, than many plays not so well.

After some work, I felt that it may be the end of the season before we learn to execute the quarterback toss play. I also felt that if we could reliably execute three basic running plays and a short pass to each side of the formation, then we would have a foundation on which to build an offense. For right-handed quarterbacks, however, a jump-pass to the left side of the formation is rather difficult. And with only eight days of training before our first game, we simply did not have time to develop a polished passing attack.

Our halfbacks needed practice in order to master certain handoff techniques. One halfback, in particular, was concerned about how I advised him to receive a handoff. He was certain that he could use the technique that he had learned the previous year. What he did not know was that in the Split-T everything happens much faster. The Spilt-T handoff technique is designed to account for the increase in speed. Nevertheless, after several attempts he was sure he could receive a handoff as he learned previously, so I reluctantly agreed to let him try it his way.

We decided to have a morning practice on Saturday, and, in the afternoon, have an officiated scrimmage to simulate game conditions.

Our Split-T Scrimmage

It was Saturday after the morning practice, and I hoped that we were ready for a scrimmage — I wanted to see what would happen. To put it bluntly, the scrimmage was a complete disaster.

For example, the halfback who resisted learning the Split-T technique for the handoff had three fumbles. In the Wilkinson system, *the success of the play depends on speed and quickness.* So time lost in the exchange of the handoff defeats the Split-T concept.

Another aspect of the Oklahoma Split-T is that *linemen do not hold their blocks.* They simply move the defensive player, either right or left, so that the halfback can cut through the quickly opening, and quickly closing, space created by the block. It follows that the ball handling techniques had to be sure and quick.

Due to many other mistakes, e.g., missed signals given by the linemen to indicate the route the halfbacks were to run, the scrimmage clearly demonstrated that if we were to be successful, then there was much work ahead.

Being an old-school coach, I try not to make or accept excuses, so I was very discouraged by our scrimmage.

After helping the manager stow the equipment, I had time to reflect on the events of the scrimmage: Only our manager, a few followers, the athletic director Squibb Wilson, and the basketball coach Pi Davis observed the scrimmage. But both Squibb and Pi left before the scrimmage was over. Perhaps they had seen enough.

Since I received feedback from neither Squibb nor Pi, I naturally believed the worst. And when I arrived at my house that lonely evening, there were no sympathizers, and possibly the natives were putting on their war paint. I felt like I was mortally wounded. My poor wife Florence had to listen to a detailed replay of the negatives. She remained calm, however, and then told me to settle down. She also adopted the positive approach by telling me that by Monday my view of the situation would improve.

It is amazing how a wife's positive views and a church members's positive views impact one's mental attitude. Sure enough, on Monday events began to move in the right direction.

During the Saturday scrimmage, I had kept a record of our mistakes.

And after the scrimmage, there were improvements, e.g., on Monday following the scrimmage the senior halfback who fumbled three times had a much improved willingness to learn. As I approached him, he asked me if I would repeat the Split-T techniques for receiving a handoff. I believe that he sensed that we needed each other. His sincerity and humility, when compared to his demeanor during the previous week, were greatly improved.

On offense we originally, during the first-four days, had six starting seniors — three linemen and three backs. But then we lost our quarterback, a junior, and two starting seniors to the Korean War, leaving us with only four starting seniors on offense and no quarterback.

I also observed that with only a week remaining before our first game, those seniors became more focused on the task at hand — getting ready for our first game.

Looking back, the veterans were certainly attached to their previous coach, and the fact that they had to learn and adapt to a new and different coaching philosophy certainly did not increase their love of the game. In short, I should have expected an adjustment period.

Monday and Tuesday Practices

Monday was the most productive practice day thus far. We were still installing the Oklahoma Split-T; and since classes were to begin on Tuesday, we were limited to one practice session per day.

At our afternoon Tuesday football practice, much to my lament (practice minutes are precious) some of our athletes were late. About one hour later, most were ready. The players did their calisthenics and wind sprints with a determined vigor. They were working like nothing bothered them.

I recall feeling hopeless and sad for the players because, at that point in time, I did not believe that much could come from their obvious enthusiasm. Nevertheless, stressing the execution of our running plays, we continued to review and improve our basic techniques and plays — running plays, our quickie, offensive tackle calls, the one pass play, and the jump pass.

Our most basic play was the so-called *quickie.* The quickie done properly sets up the *fullback-off-tackle* play and the *option* play. The option play is the quarterback option where he either keeps the ball or pitches the ball to the other halfback. As Coach Wilkinson said, "If you don't have a successful hand off (we called it quickie) the rest of the offense won't be successful." To make the defense respect the quickie play, *blocking options* are built into the design of the play. The blocking options are called using verbal signals after the offensive linemen are at the line-of-scrimmage. The key is the offensive tackle's block, which determines where the halfback (lined up behind the tackle) will look for the "hole" in the defensive line.

The tackle on the side where the play will be run has the option of determining how he can best block the defensive tackle, and then communicates his decision to the halfback.

The Role of our Tackles

If the defensive tackle is on the offensive tackle's outside (inside) shoulder, then the offensive tackle could most likely block him toward the outside (inside). Since the halfback runs behind the tackle's block, it is important that the halfback know which way his tackle is going to block, i.e., to the outside or to the inside.

But as offensive strategies and techniques increase in sophistication, adjustments on defense keep pace. For instance, today the defensive tackle may charge across your face, may stay at home, may not charge, or may do a combination of the moves. To counteract such uncertainty about what your opponent is trying to do, you simply stress that the tackle make a block toward one side or the other, and then have the halfback "run to daylight."

So the blocking decision is a decision that the tackle makes only a few seconds before the ball is snapped. Indeed, the play has been called in the huddle, the tackle goes to the line of scrimmage, the tackle looks across at the positions of the defensive players, and then decides how and in which direction he will make his block. The teaching point is that the offensive tackle must be able to "quickly make decisions about the positioning and tendencies of the defensive tackle."

The basics in 1952 were as follows: The offensive tackle's goal was to encourage the defensive tackle to set up (split out) away from his adjacent defensive lineman. The offensive tackle would do this by positioning himself a certain distance from the offensive guard, who was positioned a certain distance from the offensive center. These so-called "splits" created natural "holes" in the defensive line. Once set at the line of scrimmage, the offensive tackle had to decide, on his own, to block either to the right or to the left.

While it may sound simple, it is, in reality, not that easy. The difficulty arises because football is a team game. So once the offensive tackle decides which way that he is going to block, he must, in some sort of "secret code," alert the halfback about his decision so that the halfback can anticipate where to run.

In short, during the game, right before the ball is snapped, the tackle must convey his blocking decision without revealing where the play is going.

One method of concealing what the offensive tackle will do is that of choosing a *live color*, such as red, or blue, or green. Suppose the live color is red, and the quarterback calls the play in the huddle. Let us suppose that the quarterback calls a quick handoff to the halfback on the right side of the formation. Then all the linemen go to the line and set their splits. The left tackle may say green, but the right tackle, since the play is designed to go right, will say the live color (red). Then just before the snap, when the right halfback who is behind the right tackle is looking at the feet of the right tackle, the tackle will slightly move his left foot if he intends to block and move the defensive tackle left, or, the tackle will slightly move his right foot if he intends to block and move the defensive tackle right. Since both tackles are calling colors, and both are making slight adjustments with their feet, the defense should have difficulty breaking the code.[1]

This code keeps the defense guessing. And the last-second adjustment by the tackle is somewhat analogous to what we see when we watch Payton Manning quarterback the Colts. The idea is to see the defense first, and then make a decision that improves your chance for success.

The simplistic beauty of this scheme is that the tackles, who in some quarters are viewed as just brute strength players who contribute nothing to the mental aspects of the game, become an integral part of the offense. One might say they are not only linemen, but also part quarterback, and they must assume a large responsibility for the teams success or failure.[2]

Mike Birmingham, one of the tackles on our 1952 team, was a freshman who was also a Korean War veteran. While he was not in great condition and had only played center at the high-school level, he was an excellent tackle because he was older and wiser than most freshmen. He also was rather quick for a 6′ 1″ 200+ pound "big" man.[3]

Last Three Days of Training

We continued to review and refine the limited offensive system we had installed. We worked on executing the triple option by emphasizing the quickie and trying to perfect the quarterback pitch. We worked hard on everything

[1]In coaching this "live color scheme," I have found that it is best to select the live color on the Monday practice preceding the Saturday game; and then repeatedly use the live color as you go through your weekly drills. The repetition throughout the week minimizes the chance that the players will forget the color during the Saturday game.

[2]They must think and make the proper call, otherwise the play fails. Players appreciate a coach who places confidence in their judgment. Their morale improves, and their pride as warriors increases. Our fine young men were intelligent and caring; all they needed was for someone to believe and trust them.

[3]Before the Korean War, Mike was the regular center for Allegheny High School in Cumberland, Maryland. Earl Bruce, one-time coach at Ohio State, had started his coaching career at Allegheny High School and was this young man's high school coach. Mike also had a good sense of humor, as the following example illustrates. When he learned that he was calling the handoff play on his side of the line, and was responsible for making a call every play, Mike was elated. We kept the calls simple, using only a few colors like red, green, or blue. On one occasion, however, he called "chartreuse." Mike knew that he would be corrected, but he smiled and said he just couldn't think of another color at the time. I told him I understood how hard it was to remember green and blue. He then admitted he just got tired of hearing red, blue, etc., and wanted to call something different.

but the pitch after our Tuesday and Wednesday practice.

Since "the pitch" needed substantially more work, we decided that we would not us it in our first game. I was unsure of the safest way to execute the pitch, and evidently I was not alone in my uncertainty. Some coaches tried to pitch the ball end-over-end, while others tried to spiral the ball like a pass. I felt that we could wait until a later date to try to make the pitch a serious weapon.

There is much more to football than offense and defense. We also had to develop the punt and punt-return teams, kickoff and kickoff-return teams, and extra-point teams. The extra-point kicks were attempted at the very end of practice and usually only involved a few sessions with our center, kicker, and holder.

For the most part, our players were on all teams. For each team, i.e., offensive, defensive, punt, return, and kickoff teams, we attempted to get the best players on the field. We were fortunate in that our extra-point kicker was above average and our punter was superior.

On Thursday and Friday, we concentrated on special teams, but we did not forget to get as many repetitions as possible on the basics.

All too quickly, our first game was upon us. It was on Saturday, and we had the last eight days of training to install the Split-T. We would see if our effort paid off on Saturday.

By the end of the last week of practice prior to our first game, I had the feeling that we had come a long way. Nevertheless, because there was so much more that we had not put into the system, I was also worried about the outcome of our first game. I thought to myself, if we can just be respectable in our first game, then we shall have something that we can build on.

CHAPTER 3

First Year as College Coach
Part III: Undefeated

From Chapter 1, recall that I became Head Coach of Football at Fairmont State a few weeks prior to our 1952 season; while trying to learn Fairmont State's previous football system, I had let the quarterback be the coach for four days; mistakenly assuming that Fairmont's 1951 Split-T was the Oklahoma Split-T, I placed myself in an embarrassing situation; after the first week of practice, and just eight days prior to our first game, we lost our starting quarterback and two regulars; with only 11 practice sessions prior to the first game, I installed the Oklahoma Split-T, an offensive scheme that I had never coached.

So after 11 practice sessions of installing the Oklahoma Split-T, the Fairmont State team and its one coach, traveling in a caravan of automobiles, were "ready" to open the 1952 season. Our destination was Glenville State College.

First Game

Riding in the lead car of the caravan, I was accompanied by Squibb Wilson, Pi Davis, Tom Evans, and Emlyn Thomas.[1]

We had 25 players and one manager — here come the Falcons!

Between Squibb, Pi, Tom, Emlyn, and myself there were many conversations, and I was beginning to feel the pressure: I only had a one-year contract, and using Fairmont's 1951 Split-T system, both my team and I were inept in a public scrimmage just last week. I had also clearly indicated that whatever the outcome of the game, I would support my players and make no excuses.

On the positive side, however, I was about to test one of my long-held beliefs, namely, *The quality of a person's life is in direct proportion to their commitment to excellence, regardless of their chosen field of endeavor.*[2]

To me, any "commitment to excellence" implies a commitment to "hard work." And during the previous week of football practice, I had witnessed first hand that these fine young men who were representing Fairmont State

[1]Squibb was our Athletic Director, Pi our Head Basketball Coach, Tom a pediatrician and former Fairmont football player, and Emlyn the Sports Information Director.

[2]This statement is widely attributed to Vince Lombardi.

football had a commitment to hard work. I also had confidence that the new Split-T system was fundamentally sound.

Philosophically, I believe that the Almighty rewards those who work hard; but when we are placed in an uncomfortable situation, we may forget the power of the Almighty and our faith leaves us.

What I didn't know at game time was that the Split-T was unknown to Glenville's football coaches. They did not know what to do when our linemen took $1\frac{1}{2}$-foot splits. They moved their defensive tackles so that they lined up on the outside shoulders of our tackles. Such positioning naturally increases the distance between their adjacent players, which left gaping holes that made our basic play, the "Quickie", a powerful offensive weapon. As a result, our offense had a fine time, our defense was equal to the occasion, and Fairmont State won the game by a score of 26-to-6. We were an unusually-happy football team.

After doubting one's ability to win, there is nothing that will boost one's morale more than winning. The team instantly enjoyed an improvement in attitude — gaining confidence in their abilities, they realized that there was a chance for team success.

Our next game represented one of the greatest challenges on our schedule.

Second Game

Our second game was a home game with West Liberty State College. In 1951, the previous year, Fairmont State lost by a score of 6-to-0. And worse, in 1950 Fairmont lost by a score of 45-to-0. And from worse to worst, in the 30-year history of our football competition, Fairmont had relatively few victories over West Liberty.

The practice sessions leading up to the West Liberty game went much better because of our victory over Glenville. We had time to improve our special teams, and we entered the West Liberty game with more confidence. Our main concern? What if West Liberty does not spread their defense as Glenville had the previous week?

To prepare for that situation, I believed, because of Fairmont's close 6-to-0 loss the previous year, that if we were to win, then we would need to use some passing plays. And if we started passing, we would need the *draw play* — the fullback runs to daylight after a fake pass "draws" the defense up the field and past the line of scrimmage.

I also believed that since we did not use a single pass against our first opponent, West Liberty would be ready for our running plays. So I expected the game to feature our offensive strength, running the football, against their defensive strength, stopping the run. To make sure that we maximized our chance for success in our running game, I had to be sure that the players knew their assignments and that they could execute the plays with perfection.

On the first play of the game, West Liberty returned our kickoff to their 25-yard line. Then on the first play from scrimmage, their star halfback went off tackle and ran for a touchdown. I immediately recalled the 1950 Fairmont West Liberty game, when West Liberty won by a score of 45-to-0.

It did not take long, however, to realize that our game with West Liberty was essentially like our previous game. They spread their tackles to match our offensive tackles, creating large natural gaps to run our base play, the "Quickie." It became clear that West Liberty had not played against a team taking $1\frac{1}{2}$-foot splits, and Fairmont won by a score of 32-to-13.

The West Liberty game was one of our home games, and we had better-than-average attendance. We did not disappoint our fans.

Third Game

Our third game was at Concord. On Friday, the day before the game, we traveled approximately 100 miles and stayed overnight in Beckley, West Virginia, which is approximately 70 miles from Concord.

Because we were traveling on Friday, we had an early practice and, unfortunately, four of our freshmen, two of whom were second-team halfbacks, missed that final practice session.

Having already played two games and sustaining not one single significant injury, I decided to depart for Concord without those second-team players. So for the Concord game, the reserve halfbacks were our third-team halfbacks. I lived to regret that decision because, as it turned out, we certainly needed them.

It was Homecoming for Concord; and on Homecoming Week it is always difficult to beat the home team. The returning alumni and all the hoopla lights a fire under even the poorest of home teams; and what made it worse for Fairmont was that Concord had a fine football team.

In contrast, there were less than 25 Fairmont fans at the game — in those days of small-college football, very few fans would make a trek of over 100 miles of narrow and crooked roads to watch their team play.

Fairmont received the kickoff and, starting from their 30-yard line, drove without incident for a touchdown and added the extra point. Concord mounted a drive, but was forced to punt and pinned Fairmont back to their 10-yard line. An off-sides penalty moved the ball back to the five-yard line. With poor field position and first-and-fifteen, all I wanted was a first down.

But then the offense completed their finest drive of the entire year, going 95 yards to score a touchdown. Again, all of our plays were running plays, and we took a 14-to-0 lead in the first quarter. At that point in the game, the offense looked as good as they had the previous week against West Liberty. Then, after short series by both teams, it was clear that the play on the field was becoming very even. Neither team could score.

Late in the second quarter, however, our right halfback sustained a broken nose. Face masks were unknown in 1952, and the injury-induced bleeding was substantial, i.e., severe enough that the player could neither continue nor return to action in the second half.

So now we are using a third-team halfback. But just before halftime we got a break by recovering a fumble inside Concord's 20-yard line. We then went on to score our third touchdown and the extra point. Concord's inability to score, left us with a 21-to-0 lead, a lead which quieted the natives, homecoming fans, and alumni.

Unfortunately we had another half of football. In fact, in the second quarter we were beginning to lose momentum, and although we scored a touchdown in the second quarter it was really a lucky break. We could not move the ball consistently as we had while dominating the first quarter, and unless everything came apart we were not going to pass the ball, even though Concord had solved our limited offense — the running game.

As for our passing game, we had only thrown one short pass in $2\frac{1}{2}$ games; and, simply put, we had trouble executing passing plays.

Even without one of our regular halfbacks, we still had three starting backs and a 21-to-0 lead. So I felt that we might be able to sustain enough offense to win the game.

But early in the third quarter, our other starting halfback was injured. Again, the injury was a broken nose, and again we inserted another third-team halfback.

Near the end of the third quarter, Concord negotiated an efficient drive and scored a touchdown; but then missed the extra point, making the score 21-to-6 in Fairmont's favor. That drive motivated the fans and increased Concord's momentum. Their offense was rolling, and their defense had shut us out in the second half.

If we were to win, then our offense, slowed in the second quarter and now almost inept, had to generate something. But how? We only had two of our starting backs, our quarterback and our fullback.

And then it became worse. Our quarterback, Blaine Morton, suffered an ankle injury and his back-up had never taken a college-game snap. On the positive side, our reserve quarterback was an intelligent young man who could perform all of the mechanics of the position, i.e., he would not hurt the team with mishandled balls or mental errors. But Blaine also played defensive end, and his replacement would have to do his very best.

So we were down to only one or our starting backs, our fullback Jim Cherocci. How do we generate offense? Jim was a fine athlete, and except for his speed, he was a great back. But most importantly, Jim was an outstanding punter. It turned out that his punting was our best weapon for that extremely-long second half.

With one quarter remaining, Concord was in complete control. Could we possibly hold on? Early in the fourth quarter, Concord powered their way to a second touchdown and added the extra point, making the score 21-to-13.

Half way through the fourth quarter, Concord's fullback had sparked their offense — he looked unstoppable. Fairmont's offense, however, could not make a first down. We were using as much time between plays as possible, and we were depending on our punter to keep them in poor field position. Our defense made a couple of stops, and our punter did a masterful job.

We had a tiger by the tail: Fanatic fans were standing and stomping their feet. Every call was challenged. We faced a super-charged football team. Could we hold on?

Concord had the ball and they showed their dominance. They charged through our defense and scored their third touchdown. The extra point was missed and Fairmont, at 21-to-19, was clinging to a slight lead. With five huge remaining-minutes on the clock, we were weary and wounded. We had no offense. We were totally depending on our defense and kicking game. We received the kickoff, and continued our quest to run out the clock.

Again, however, we did not make a first down but our punter helped by making a long punt. Then after two first downs, Concord was forced to punt with only two huge remaining-minutes on the clock.

I felt that if our offense could hold the ball for one minute, and if we got another good punt, then we could win. Our depleted offense, however, could not move the ball, and Concord called enough timeouts to ensure themselves that they would have a chance to win the game. Our punter then made a long punt and it was once again up to our defense. Our defense held, and we won that injury-inflicted hard-fought game by the score of 21-to-19. In general, those kinds of wins really build team character.

Fourth Game

Undefeated with three of our backs injured, we were preparing to play Davis & Elkins College. We had concerns not only about our football strategy, but also about the health of our football players. At the practices leading up to the game all of our young men, especially those who were injured in the previous game, showed true grit by neither complaining nor making excuses.

Our part-time physician, Harry Flemming, who was also excited about the team, provided medical care for our two halfbacks with nose injuries. Since face masks were not available in 1952, Harry used cotton and tape to provide stabilization. And even when informed that a second injury to the nose could be rather serious, both halfbacks insisted on playing. Our quarterback had a swollen ankle, but he did not develop a limp.

Perhaps it is not a truism, but it seems that injured athletes recover more quickly when they are needed for an upcoming high-stakes game. In our case, all three of our injured backs played in the Davis & Elkins game.

As for an adjustment in our strategy, the lesson I learned from the Concord game was that we had to expand our offense. So while we continued to work on the basics, we added new formations.

In one formation, we positioned our right halfback outside of our right end, thereby providing an improved blocking angle for *outside* or *end-run* plays. Such a formation would help our quarterback feature his running skills — he was a powerful runner with better than average speed.

We also worked on the details surrounding the execution of certain plays. In particular, to gain an advantage at the line of scrimmage, we focused on our *starting count strategy.*

Typically, we used the *non-rhythmic starting count* — if the ball is to be snapped on say the third sound, the quarterback may make the first two sounds in rapid succession, then pause, and then make the third sound. Such a non-rhythmic count does not allow the defense to anticipate when the ball will be snapped, and thereby gain an advantage at the line of scrimmage.

Because of the physical and mental intensity of football, players tend to wear down, and when they become tired, their acumen decreases. So late in a game, it is difficult for your players to concentrate and listen closely to a non-rhythmic count. To avoid the increased likelihood that your players will make a mistake and miss the snap count, a football team must regularly practice their non-rhythmic count, so much so that it does not require a lot of concentration.

I believe that the teaching point on the value of the non-rhythmic count is that if both teams have athletes of similar strengths, then whenever a defense can anticipate the starting count they will attack the offensive player, possibly beating him on his first movement, and greatly decrease any chance for a successful block. On the other hand, if the offensive linemen get the first movement and they are properly trained in blocking, the chance for executing a successful block is greatly increased.

So we regularly worked on the non-rhythmic count aspect of our offense. During our sprint drills, e.g., we would run all the linemen at the same time and have different linemen call the snap signal with a non-rhythmic count. We observed who the linemen were that would either jump or move too soon or too late, and those linemen would be required to run extra laps around our 440-yard track.

We were also dedicated to perfecting another starting count. We called it the *quarterback goose.* In this case, the quarterback makes no sound. Instead, the quarterback would wait until the entire team was set at the line of scrimmage, then pause for a second, maybe looking left or right, and then *goose the center* with his hand, which communicated to the center that he was to snap the ball. The goal is to never let the defense start at the same time as the offense, i.e., in football vernacular, the offense wants to keep the defense "off balance." *A quarterback goose is especially effective when the offense needs at most a yard.* So we practiced this situation over and over.

The key teaching techniques are (1) only four team members are initially involved in the goose — the two guards, the quarterback, and the center; (2) the other seven players are not to move until the play is in progress. The reason for teaching (2) is simply that when fewer players are involved, there is less chance for a false move, which would negate the play. The goose technique may be used on any occasion when the offense needs at most a yard. If a team is properly prepared for such a short-yard situation, the defense will not beat the offense on the snap count, and if the team has a powerful quarterback, it is most probable that the goose play will be successful.

While the *goose the center* and the *non-rhythmic starting count* concepts sound almost trivial, the task of synchronizing 11 players so that they execute these concepts flawlessly in the middle of a heated football game is no simple matter. It is only through repeated practicing that 11 individual players will take the next step and become a team.

It turned out that we needed the goose play during our game with Davis & Elkins College. At halftime, the score was tied at 0-to-0. The defensive struggle continued into the second half, with the score still tied at 0-to-0. The critical play occurred while we had the ball at the 50 yard line, where we faced a fourth down and needed one yard for a first down.

We called the quarterback sneak on the goose. Since we had dedicated so much practice time to the "quarterback goose," I felt confident that the call was not a gamble.

The fans knew the down and distance. There is a rumble throughout the crowd, and I knew fully well that I would be the goat if the play failed, especially if we lose the game because of the play. In any case, we ran the play; and our quarterback, Blaine Morton, not only made the needed yard, but he went 50 yards for a touchdown. After that the game changed, and Fairmont State went on to win by a score of 25-to-0. Moreover, more than staying undefeated, our previously injured halfbacks and quarterback sustained no further injuries. And so going into our fifth game, Fairmont State was once again at full strength.

Fifth Game

Our fifth opponent was Salem College. In 1952 Salem College was a Seven Day Adventist Institution that celebrated their Holy Day on Saturday. So our game was scheduled one day early, on Friday afternoon.

Since our team was in good physical shape, we did not need the extra day for rest. Nevertheless, a "hard-to-believe" situation arose on Thursday that involved our starting right tackle, Mike Birmingham.

Mike was a freshman who was also a Korean War Veteran. I realized something was wrong when Mike did not show up for practice on Thursday. I learned from his roommate that he had an infection, and that he was in so much pain that he could not even sit in a chair.

So after practice I stopped by his apartment and witnessed first hand his suffering and severe pain. The swelling and redness was obvious, and while I am not trained in the medical sciences, I knew that he needed immediate attention. My first thought was of my next-door neighbor, Claude Lawson. Claude was my former classmate at Fairmont State and a locally-practicing surgeon. So I called Claude and explained the situation.

He was just leaving his office and indicated that he would be at Mike's apartment in a few minutes. After he arrived and examined Mike, he said that the area of concern needed immediate attention. With medical equipment that he had brought with him, Claude positioned Mike so that he could make the proper incision.

Then, in Mike's apartment, the infected area was lanced. It was fortunate, and now somewhat humorous, that Claude was wearing his glasses — the instant release of pressure propelled a substantial, and I mean substantial, viscous substance directly toward Claude's eyes, which were protected by his glasses.

He then instructed Mike how to position his body so that the wound would drain. This experience had a happy ending when Mike told us that he felt instant relief.

But I then got even better news, after Claude bandaged Mike's wound he indicated that he would see Mike the following morning, Friday, and that there was no reason why Mike could not play in the Friday afternoon game with Salem.

I had dismissed even the possibility of Mike being able to play in less than 24 hours. In addition, any concerns about further aggravation of his infection were dismissed by Claude's explanation that since the wound would be properly monitored and protected, that Mike would not have to worry.

Sure enough, the next day Mike said he felt great and that he would play in the game. He also indicated that his father was going to be at the game. That afternoon, I met his kind and modest father, who was very supportive of his son and his son's team.

On that same day, Fairmont State went on to win the Salem College game by a score of 33-to-7.

Final Game of 1952 Season

Fairmont States's last game of the 1952 season was against a fine and a very strong California State team from Western Pennsylvania. We played the game on California State's home field. It had rained all during the day prior to game day, on game day the sky looked threatening, but we only had off-and-on sprinkles.

To set the scene, it was simply a dreary, gray November sky, two teams with excellent records were playing a hard fought football game, and there were only a small crowd of spectators. Although we did not expect the weather conditions and a small crowd of fans to impact the game, it turned out that these conditions gave our team an advantage.[3]

Under these wet and muddy conditions, California's chief offensive weapon was their huge ($6'\,2''$ and about 220 lbs) fullback Nemo Natali. He was not unusually fast, but he was quick with good balance and plenty of power. In my mind, the slippery turf somewhat diminished some of his natural talent. In particular, he could not start as quickly as was possible on a dry turf, and his ability to make quick cuts to evade tacklers was definitely reduced.

Of course, a wet and muddy football also restricts both the receivers and the passer. To me, the weather greatly diminished any advantages that California State might have had over Fairmont State.

The game quickly settled into a defensive struggle, neither team could mount a serious drive during the first half. The second half started like the first half ended, i.e., it was a strictly defense contest.

Early in the fourth quarter, however, Fairmont started to have some success on offense. A drive, consisting of mostly-short grudgingly-allowed gains, led Fairmont to California State's two-yard line. On our fourth-down play, Fairmont's quarterback ran a sweep and barely made it into the end zone. We used the formation with a split back that we introduced during the practice week following the Concord game. That was the first time that that formation had been called, and it worked — at the start of the play the split-out halfback had an advantageous blocking angle on the defensive line backer, and the subsequent block gave the quarterback just enough room to score the touchdown.

California State had an exceptionally well-coached football team, and such teams do not give up. With about seven minutes remaining and down 7-to-0, California State was ready to make a statement. Sure enough, they came roaring back. Seemingly supercharged, they were driving toward our end zone. Contrasting their drive toward our end zone with our touchdown drive, I felt that their drive was more assertive. They were making first

[3]In the 1950s, small-college football games never seemed to draw very large crowds. With an undefeated season on the line, however, I expected a larger crowd.

downs with large chunks of yards by dominating our defense.

Then with less than two minutes to play, California State was facing fourth down on Fairmont's two-yard line. I knew their big fullback was ready to finish their drive. However, Fairmont had a two-time all conference guard, Dale Hounshell.[4]

Everyone knew that their huge fullback "Nemo Natiali" would carry the ball.[5]

Nemo was going to be a handful, and then came the crucial play: Natali was handed the ball and he was headed to his right, toward Fairmont's huge defensive left tackle, Clem Dawson. Clem did his job of filling the hole where Nemo was trying to run. The big fullback Nemo and the huge tackle Clem met, and Nemo was slowed, and actually momentarily stopped, but Nemo's momentum carried him toward the end zone.

Ordinarily, we told our players to tackle at the waist, but in this case a waist tackle on Nemo would allow him to fall forward over the goal line. Just in time, Dale Hounshell arrived and quickly displayed his exceptional and outstanding ability — at the goal line Dale grabbed Nemo's arm and shoulder; Dale then pulled Nemo back away from the goal line so that the ball neither broke the plane nor crossed the goal line.

To this day, I can see, in my mind's eye, Dale Hounshell holding on and pulling with all his strength. He was determined to keep the great Nemo from ruining an unbelievable undefeated season for Fairmont State.[6]

Reflections on The Final Game

On their rocky road to a perfect season, the 1952 Fairmont State team faced unbelievable adversity. Examples of the adversity permeate the entire season.

Even two days prior to the final game the right tackle, Fred Bonvenuto (who shared playing time with, and was the back-up to our starting right tackle, Mike Birmingham) told me that he had been drafted and had to report for duty on Saturday, the day of our final game.

Fred was fine young man who had been a center in high school. He had no previous college experience and he tried out for college football only as a senior. Fred had a great attitude and he was very intelligent and cooperative. Just like Mike, Fred shared and accepted his role on our team, and he made

[4]Dale made All-Conference at the end of the 1952 season to become Fairmont's only 3-time All-Conference selection. He stood 5′ 9″ and weighed 175 lbs. He was both extremely quick and extremely strong. These attributes along with his *football sense*, an ability to locate the football, allowed him to get to the ball quicker than any player I have ever seen.

[5]Nemo Natali had played at Monessen High School in Pennsylvania, where Nemo's counterpart for Fairmont, Jim Cherocii, was Natali's backup.

[6]The 1952 undefeated season was the first undefeated season in the school's history.

a huge contribution. What was sad, however, was the fact that Fred could not delay his induction by even one day.

So for the final game, the team had only one reserve freshman tackle — a "hard-nosed" football player who stepped in at defensive tackle and helped his team go undefeated. As the only coach, I had to focus on teaching the starting players, and so the back-up players were less prepared for specific assignments. Nevertheless, even though our loss of the first alternate tackle was a major blow, especially in such a high-stakes game, the team prevailed as they had at numerous times during the season. With less than 10 Fairmont faithful attending the final game, the celebration of going undefeated was mostly a team celebration. So, on a cold, rainy, and dreary day on a mud covered field, those young men finally vented their enthusiasm and enjoyed the fruits of their labor. They even carried their followers off the field. I wish I could have carried each of them off the field.

Fairmont State was declared the 1952 *West Virginia Conference Football Champion.*[7]

[7]Fairmont State had not received that honor since 1934, when Jasper Colebank was Head Coach. The complete list of years (from 1908, the first year that Fairmont State fielded a football team, through 2006) that Fairmont State was declared West Virginia Conference Football Champion follows: 1934, 1952, 1957, 1959, 1960, 1964, 1965, 1967, 1969, 1973, 1974, 1979, 1981, 1988, 1996, and 2000. Fairmont State was also invited to play in a National Association of Intercollegiate Athletics (NAIA) playoff tournament in the following years: 1965, 1967, 1981, and 1988. Fairmont State also played in the Shrine Bowl Game in 1973 and 1974; and the Coal Bowl Game in 1979. The Fairmont State Football team was declared the 1967 NAIA Champion.

CHAPTER 4

The Championship Saga

Every team of every sport starts every season with the hope of winning a championship. Most, however, do not truly believe they will do so. Likewise, fans and followers wish for championships, but they also have their doubts.

Successful coaches and players must believe that they can achieve almost anything that has been achieved in a similar situation; and that together they can possibly exceed past performances. It is my observation that it is these kinds of players and coaches who produce the championships and record setters.

Undefeated in 1957, no NAIA Playoff

With Fairmont State as a member of the National Association of Intercollegiate Athletics (NAIA), its 1957 football team posted a perfect season of seven wins and no losses. We had scheduled eight games, but unfortunately we only played seven because one of our opponents had dropped football, and we were unsuccessful in our efforts to fill that void. So having only seven games on our schedule, it seemed understandable that we would not be selected by the NAIA to play for a national championship.

Undefeated in 1959, no NAIA Playoff

With nine wins and no loses, the 1959 Fairmont State football team had a perfect season. While the NAIA ranked all teams, only the top four were then scheduled to play for the NAIA National Championship. The final rankings appeared in the last week in November, and Fairmont State with its perfect season was not ranked in the top 25. In contrast, one of the Texas teams with a 7-and-3 record was ranked number seven.

Our first goal in 1959 was to win our Conference, the West Virginia Intercollegiate Athletic Conference (WVIAC). We had accomplished that goal, and by the end of the season, we were one of only a few NAIA teams to have an undefeated season.

Because of our relatively low final ranking, it was clear that we needed to better understand how these rankings were determined. So I contacted Al Duer, the NAIA Commissioner, to ask why our team had not received *a single vote* in support of ranking Fairmont in the top 25.

He justified the Rating Committee's decision by stating that there was no way to determine Fairmont State's team strength because he believed our Conference teams had no substantial record of games played outside of our league. Disappointed to say the least, we felt that the entire WVIAC Conference was spurned — we had accomplished the rather rare feat of going undefeated in a league we perceived as very strong. I was distraught.

Nevertheless, Commissioner Duer and I talked about contacting the coach of the 1959 NAIA Championship team, namely, Frank "Muddy" Waters, who coached at Hillsdale College in Michigan. We also discussed the possibility of scheduling a game between Fairmont and Hillsdale. Indeed, I recall Commissioner Duer asking about full football scholarships at Fairmont. And after I told him that we had none, he replied that Hillsdale had 48 such scholarships.

He also inquired about the number of coaches on my staff. I told the Commissioner that at Fairmont there are only two football coaches — my line coach, William Floyd, and myself. His reply was that Hillsdale had eight coaches. Even worse for Fairmont football, Bill Floyd was also the head wrestling coach, taught an 18-hour course load, and served as Director of our Men's Dormitory.[1]

Fairmont meets Hillsdale in 1961

Commissioner Duer said he thought I might be making a mistake by playing such a powerful opponent, and as it turned out, he was right. Coach Waters was merciful.

In more detail, Fairmont and Hillsdale played their first game in 1961; the final score was Hillsdale 56 Fairmont State 6. And if Coach Waters had not removed his first team from the game, he could have named the score.

We had 14 blue-chip players, but only 7 played in that game. Had the other seven played, however, it would not have mattered. Perhaps the score would have been a bit closer, but Hillsdale had a great team, and we validated the fact that the NAIA rankings were well founded.

An Epoch in Fairmont Football History?

I believe that the Fairmont game with Hillsdale may be viewed as an *epoch* in the long history of the Fairmont State Football Program. That is, the Hillsdale game was a notable event that marked the beginning of a remarkable or noteworthy period in the history of Fairmont State football.

Indeed, *prior to the Hillsdale game* Fairmont had basically limited itself to competing with mostly in-state colleges; the ultimate goal being the WVIAC Championship. But *after the Hillsdale game* Fairmont had stepped onto the national stage, trying to compete with arguably the nation's best

[1]Coach Floyd left Fairmont after two years to obtain his Doctorate, and then accepted a position at La Cross, a Wisconsin University.

NAIA football team. So Fairmont State football could move in one of two directions: We could either return our focus to the WVIAC championship, or, take the necessary steps to successfully compete at the national level.

One of my goals in life was to see Fairmont State football successfully compete at the national level. There were no secrets about my point of view. In fact, when I first met Easton Feaster, then President of Fairmont State, I posed the following question, "*What kind of football program do you desire*?" His reply,, "*The best.*" At that point in time we were on the same page. And I had worked to do exactly that, i.e., make the football program "the best."

My understanding of the President's statement was that *the best* meant *the best in the nation.* To achieve such a goal, however, I knew that there would be times when we could not "do business as usual." Simply put, things would have to change, and change is usually met with some resistance.

One such instance of resistance involved the Hillsdale game (played at Hillsdale). We traveled to Hillsdale and played that game at no cost to Fairmont State because Hillsdale guaranteed Fairmont $1200. After returning to campus, I met with Easton and he inquired about whether we were going to host Hillsdale at Fairmont. I said yes, and informed him that Hillsdale had guaranteed us $1200, and that I had the $1200 check. But when I indicated that I had made a similar commitment to Hillsdale for a return game, the President posed two questions: *Isn't Hillsdale out of our class*?, and, *Where will we get the* $1200? I replied that Hillsdale as our host gave us Class A treatment; and I answered his question with the question, "*How could I not offer Hillsdale a similar package*?" — I felt sure that playing the top team in the NAIA would assure us a packed house and would therefore provide sufficient funds. The President's reply was to suggest that unless we could come up the funds we could not guarantee the $1200.

Humbled with a bruised ego, I talked with the Hillsdale coach, "Muddy" Waters, telling him about the situation. He told me not to worry and in a few days he solved the problem: Flint (Michigan) Lions Club agreed to sponsor the game, and we could use a local-to-Flint 20,000 seat stadium. The Lions Club would pay us $3000 which would be split $1800 to $1200 with Fairmont receiving the former and Hillsdale the latter.

Thankfully, my struggle to see Fairmont State compete on the national level took birth at the 1961 Hillsdale game. And it turned out that my life-time goal of seeing Fairmont State *successfully* compete at the national level was realized six years later, when Fairmont State was honored as the 1967 National NAIA Champion.

Turning Defeat into a Path to Victory

In 1961 when Hillsdale defeated Fairmont 56-to-6, one could rightly say that the Fairmont State football program really *took it on the chin.* But looking back, that day may now be viewed as a *day of awakening* that put us on a course that would take us to the 1967 NAIA National Championship.

They say that experience is the best teacher, and the experience of that single game taught us that for Fairmont State to compete for a championship, changes had to be made: Instead of 14 blue-chip players, we needed 25; and we also needed at least four coaches. Of course, these are ultimately decisions that only the Administration can make because funding is always limited. But as coaches and players, we can decide to work harder and work smarter.

Since we did not have scholarships, we had to work harder with the athletes we did have. We had to install programs that concentrate on strength, on endurance, on techniques, on speed, and on anything that would help us improve. We had to do a better job of evaluating high school athletes — with experience, one can identify the high school football players who can produce at the college/university level.

There are many potentially good athletes who may not have played on a winning high-school team. Such boys may be slow to develop or simply lack weight. In the latter case, one can "beef up" such young boys with a proper conditioning program. It is my experience that there are plenty of good athletes who are overlooked. Such young athletes are simply gems that only need polishing.

At Fairmont State in the 1960s, I had to focus on such developmental programs because we had no other choice. If my views were true, then we could go out and prove it. Of course it would have been nice to have 8 assistants and 48 scholarships, but until I could make the case, I had no other options. I knew what I had, and I had to make a choice, either complain and be miserable, or work harder.

What and How Could We Change?

We were beginning to make progress because we were at least trying to determine how to develop a good program. In the late 1950s, we had been motivated by Louisiana State's Chinese Bandits. Indeed, the team speed of Louisiana State, especially on the defensive side where the pursuit to the ball was exceptional, taught us that speed was critical. Simply put, the words of Paul Bear Bryant, namely *Luck follows speed*, took on new meaning.

How can one develop speed? Chuck Coker at Occidental College provided one answer in an article that appeared in *Scholastic Magazine*.

In addition, following that 1961 humiliating defeat at Hillsdale College, we knew we had to increase the strength of each player, the size of our defensive and offensive linemen, and the size of our linebackers. To address these concerns of speed, size, and strength, we initiated programs at Fairmont State, but they were poorly organized — only a few of our dedicated and mature football players worked hard enough to realize measurable results.

But if we were to contend for a national championship, these programs had to be in place and all of our players had to be involved.

Fortune smiled on Fairmont State football when we went to Morgantown, West Virginia, to watch West Virginia University (WVU) play Navy. The indomitable Roger Staubach, quarterback of Navy, put on a great show of football savvy. Navy had height and weight limits, and appeared and looked very small. West Virginia had oversized athletes; huge players who looked unbeatable for this small Navy team. By halftime, however, Navy was ahead of WVU by 35-to-0.

It was one of the finest displays of speed and execution I had ever seen. How quickly Navy's offensive line executed blocks, how fast the defense got to the point of attack. It was amazing.

But I was at the game for the purpose of improving the Fairmont State program, and generally if one is determined to improve, they will occasionally get a break. Mine came because I attended the game with the father, Lionel Bickel, of the Navy's back-up quarterback, Bruce Bickel.

Finding Solutions at the Naval Academy

Perhaps it was my enthusiasm for that performance, and my indication of how I would like my players to execute like Navy, that encouraged my friend Lionel to ask if I would be interested in a visit to the Naval Academy. Wow, I could see the Naval football program first-hand.

Lionel made arrangements not only for me, but also for one of my players — my fine sophomore fullback Roy Jackson who had great potential.[2]

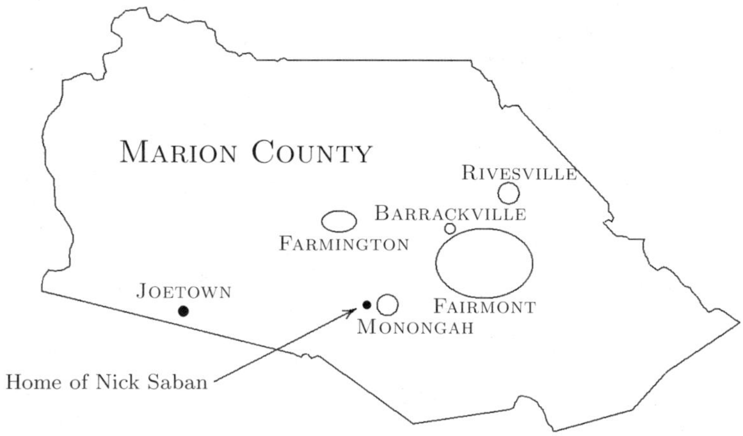

The trip to the Academy was the beginning of a golden era for football at Fairmont State, an era that would see FSU as an NAIA National Champion.

[2]Both Roy Jackson and Nick Saban attended Monongah High School in Monongah, West Virginia. Roy followed Nick by about seven years. Nick Saban currently coaches the University of Alabama, and he also coached LSU and the NFL Miami Dolphins.

We learned that all freshmen attend the Naval Academy for orientation *in the summer prior to their first year.* In particular, the football players are assigned to a physical conditioning program of 10 weeks of intense strength and speed drills. After the program is completed, they are ready to combat veterans and upperclassmen. Not only do they get stronger and quicker, they also compete with less chance for injury. And when you can compete on near even terms as to strength, this does wonders for your confidence — there is much less chance for the freshman to give up because he is discouraged and defeated. I recall how the Navy trainer, Red Romo, had the program organized to get maximum results. He was developing speed and agility in the young players.[3]

Weight Training and Agility

For some reason, I believed heavy weights could make the athlete muscle bound. I had incorrectly reasoned that if you are "muscled up" as a young man, you couldn't be effective because you couldn't move quickly enough, say moving quickly to the right or left.

But prior to our visit to the Navy Academy, a trip to a Coaching Clinic in Harrisburg, Pennsylvania, and a lecture and demonstration by Bob Hoffman, who developed the York Barbell, convinced me that you needed heavy weights not only to develop strength, but also agility.

I asked Bob if using heavy weights would possibly make an athlete muscle bound and unable to move. At the time, there was a "muscled up" young man next to Hoffman who was in shorts, and it was easy to envision my own linebackers looking like this superior specimen in shoulder pads and football equipment. But I feared for his agility.

Bob Hoffman removed all doubts: "Are you worried about his ability to move and his agility?" he asked. Then he called his demonstrator over and said to the young man, "Do a backward flip (somersault)." No shoes, just barefoot, he bent his knees and zoom, he did a perfectly executed backward somersault.

The lad hardly finished when Bob said, "Do a forward somersault." Zoom, he did it gracefully perfect. I asked Bob, "Does he have any eligibility left?" I was disappointed that this young specimen had never played football — he was a gymnast. (I thought about some of the Fairmont State football players who could benefit by following the program that produced this fabulous athlete.)

---

[3]The value of increasing speed and agility in young players was clearly realized by Paul Dietzel's LSU Chinese Bandits, where the conditioning coach, Alvin Roy, had success.

Starting Our Weight-Training Program

After the demonstration by Bob Hoffman, I couldn't wait to get home to get started on a program for FSU football. But we didn't get it right until we visited the Naval Academy. It was there that we found out that it was necessary to have a Summer Conditioning Program for the freshmen and the veteran athletes who need special attention. We set up a study hall for the freshmen that were in summer school. Freshmen went to classes in the mornings, conditioned in the afternoon, and went to study hall from 6-to-8PM four nights a week. We had an organized program that required full-time participation for 10 weeks in the summer.

But it was the early 1960s; and there was a downside: The idea of year-around conditioning and so much emphasis on one sport was viewed as *over emphasis* — the athlete and the coach will burn out. And since the administration was necessarily conservative, but rather wise, they believed in a balanced program of academics and athletics. Moreover, too much of one detracted from the other. And it is very difficult to argue that "over emphasis" will not cause a harmful imbalance. In addition, an "over emphasis" may foster a bad relationship with the academic faculty, especially if it deprives them of necessary funds.

On the upside, however, it was the academic success of our freshmen that cemented our positive relationship with the faculty.

Personally, knowing that there are two sides to any issue, I see coaches demanding much of their athletes and the athletes demanding more financial aid or more concessions because of the extra time spent on the sport. As a coach, you feel compelled to ask for more help than can actually be delivered. The coach that gets along with the Principal/President and Faculty is the coach who is most likely to succeed. Coaches definitely need faculty support, and, at Fairmont State we were able to accomplish two of our goals:

- Provide our athletes financial help with work scholarships and grants.
- Add another full-time coach and a student coach to the coaching staff.

The implementation of our program required work. Our athletic director was somewhat reluctant to join our effort. As he said, "The Navy gives financial help to their candidates; who would finance our summer program?" My view was that the parents of the athletes would help support such a program.

The program was slow in developing. In 1961, two years after we were 9-and-0 and unranked, we fell to a lower rating, and by 1963 we were 3-and-5.

Nevertheless, we were so impressed with the Naval Academy summer program and what it had accomplished that we continued to pursue every avenue so as to get a similar program at Fairmont State.

In my mind, selling the program to the parents was the key issue. Where possible, I talked to parents face-to-face. I told them we had limited financial aid, but I knew they wanted the best for their sons, and that if the parents would help with the finances, then their sons would be in a first class program. On the positive side, these freshmen athletes would take only six hours in each summer-time quarter of 5 weeks, a schedule that would ease them into college-level academics. We spent the spring of 1964 talking to the prospective athletes and their parents, stressing the fact that we were wanting our fine young men to graduate in four years.

Eight-and-one in 1964, no NAIA Playoff

After our 1963 3-and-5 season, red flags were flying, we had to operate in emergency mode. Good coaches operate in emergency mode at all times.

So following a robust winter program that focused on strength and agility, we had an excellent spring program that emphasized endurance, speed, and quickness. When athletes see progress, they get excited, and they will continue as long as progress occurs.

Our summer program was as mandatory as we could make it, given that it occurred during summer school. We did not want our young men to lose any of the additional strength, agility, and speed that they had acquired since last season. Most of these young men, especially the ones who needed additional work, attended the summer program. The result was an eight-win one-loss season, which gave us another WVIAC Championship, but again there was no invitation to the NAIA playoffs — in 1964 all four NAIA top-ranked teams were undefeated.

Weight-Training Program Improves

Following the 1964 season, we were ready to put in the final step. So we started with the 1965 freshmen. These freshmen football athletes were required to attend summer school and be in the summer conditioning program before they could participate in the fall football season and be eligible for varsity status.

We could not expect or require, however, the two assistant coaches to give up their summer with no compensation. Nevertheless, one of the two coaches volunteered.

In fact, because of his previous station where a similar program was used, he was anxious to get started, and he volunteered to work all summer in our program. His enthusiasm and expertise changed what was a good summer program into an excellent one. He had been head coach at a high school in Clewiston, Florida; and he had attended football clinics where most of the great coaches of the time had appeared on the program.

Ray Graves, head coach of the University of Florida, had divulged his conditioning program and my assistant coach had paid close attention to the proper techniques used in handling the iron weights. Without this knowledge, an inexperienced athlete could do more harm than good. This fine assistant had played one year at Fairmont State after two years at Potomac State, WV; and he was a member of our 1959 undefeated team. His name was Joseph "Joe" Bundy.

In general, a new coach who is concerned about using weight training should consult someone who has had experience. Today, many individuals are well versed in the proper use of weights — it is most likely that most coaches, even down to the junior high level, have sufficient knowledge to begin a *safe* weight-training program. While the implementation of such programs are possible, a work schedule of 18-hour work days and six-day work weeks throughout the year is required.

With our 1964 8-and-1 record and with most of the key players returning, the coaches and the entire squad were looking forward to the 1965 season. The 1964 program of conditioning was not totally complete, so in 1965 we asked even more of our players. That is, we asked some of the upper classmen who we were going to need, all of the freshmen, and the Jr. College transfers to attend summer school and be in the summer conditioning program under our supervision.

Recall the saying *Out of sight, out of mind* — if an athlete is not in a program, he will not be disciplined enough to work really hard at conditioning. However, when he is in a supervised program, his progress can be tracked, he will compete with his teammates, and he will give his best.

The summer of 1965 was, to date, our best summer of conditioning. Although we may not have accomplished all of our goals, we felt like we were ready to compete with anyone. And then, on the second day of our fall football camp, with 35 freshmen and our lettermen who completed our summer training program on the field, we received a call from Mo Scarry, the Head Football Coach at Waynesburg College in Pennsylvania. Coach Scarry wanted to schedule a practice game with Fairmont State.[4]

Waynesburg College was a private institution not affiliated with any league, thus they set their own rules. There are general rules all colleges and universities have to follow, such as academic progress and grade point averages, but starting their fall practice and the number of days you are permitted to practice is their prerogative. Fairmont State, on the other hand, being a state school and a member of the state WVIAC conference, has specific rules that all league members must follow. After I told coach Scarry that Fairmont already had a scrimmage game scheduled for the end of the

[4]Waynesburg had won the NAIA Championship in 1964, and Mo Scarry was Waynesburg's new head coach. Mo had been the offensive line coach for the Cleveland Browns when Paul Brown, the Head Coach of the Cleveland Browns, was fired. It is doubtful Scarry would have accepted the coaching job at a college as small as Waynesburg had he had time to consider other opportunities.

second week of camp, he asked why we couldn't have a game with them this week on Saturday. I explained that we were only in our second day, that we had not yet installed an offense, and that in about a week we would be ready to scrimmage.

In what seemed to be a condescending tone, he insisted that Fairmont State football players were tough and ready to scrimmage. While the idea of a scrimmage after only five days of practice had not crossed my mind, I asked Mo to give me a minute to see if my assistant coaches thought that we could be ready to scrimmage in five days. At first blush, they said no.

Putting the condescension aside, however, we were nevertheless anxious to see how we were doing and how we would compete against a quality team. We knew our athletes were in top physical shape, so injuries should not be a problem; and we knew we would not have much offense, but we only needed basics. What I did not tell my assistant coaches, however, was that Waynesburg was in their third week of practice and that they already had one scrimmage game. So somewhat reluctantly we agreed to get ready for a scrimmage by the end of the week. We surmised that if we played the game a week earlier than anticipated, then we would work harder to get ready. In addition, our athletes, most of whom had been working hard all summer, would rather play than "go through drills and dull practice sessions."

On the following Saturday, after five days of practice, the Waynesburg College football team arrived at our campus. They had a few maxi-sized athletes, which I believe temporarily intimidated a few of our players. We were trying to get to where Waynesburg had already been. They have a coach who was the line coach for the great Paul Brown, while our coaches played and coached at Fairmont State. I considered the question, *Could it be that we are out of our class*? The Waynesburg squad had that swagger-of-confidence, and they were sounding off like pros. I must admit, the stakes seemed so very high, and I had never felt that way before any game.

Many things entered my mind during warm ups. I recalled what Al Duer had told me when I wanted to play Hillsdale College — we might have a hard time competing at a high level. Then we lost by the score of 56-to-6. I also remembered telling my athletes that they could accomplish most anything if they worked hard enough. And since the players and the coaches had done their part, serious failure could destroy their confidence. With the tools we had, there was no more we could do.

But we did not fail. Neither team was able to dominate the other. The game ended with each team scoring two touchdowns. The rules of the scrimmage were as follows: Each team got the ball on their own 20, and if you did not make a first down, the other team got the ball; otherwise, the team that began on offense retained the ball for 16 plays when they continued to make first downs.

At one point during the scrimmage, we were on Waynesburg's one-yard line when we exhausted our limit of 16 plays. After the scrimmage, we realized that we could play with anyone in our class. As we were leaving the field and discussing the events of the game, I observed that Mo Scarry had a slightly different and not so dominating demeanor.

The Fairmont State coaches received (indirectly) a fantastic compliment —as we were walking off the field, Coach Scarry asked me how many days we had practiced. I replied that this was our 6th day. He said, "You are a G.D. Liar." I knew we had impressed him, and there was no reason to tell him we had been weight lifting and running all summer.

As to my personal feelings about Coach Scarry's statement, one must place his comment in the context of a hard-fought football game. Never forget that most coaches are former players, and just because a player turns out to be a coach does not mean that he has lost his edge. In summary, I knew that he was giving our team and our coaches a compliment.

As to the caliber of the Waynesburg athletes, the following year Waynesburg's quarterback, Theofideles, and offensive tackle, Regetti, played for the Washington Redskins and the Cleveland Browns, respectively.

Undefeated in 1965, in NAIA Playoff

We went on to finish the 1965 season undefeated with eight wins; and then lady luck smiled on us, or did she?

We were hoping that the NAIA would rank us among the top four teams, which would ensure that Fairmont would receive an NAIA playoff bid. The rankings that came out the week following our final game had Fairmont at number eight; and with three weeks remaining in the regular season, the rankings could change. Realistically, however, we knew our chances were slim.

So we terminated practice sessions because we could not keep our team practicing with only a slim chance that enough teams would lose. Some of our football players also participated in basketball and wrestling, and those programs were already underway. When the final ratings were published, we were ranked number seven, meaning that our season was over.

Surprisingly, a few days later we received a call from Al Duer, Executive Secretary of the NAIA, who indicated that several of the teams ranked above Fairmont State would not be able to raise the necessary funds to participate. So in 1965, we backed into the NAIA playoffs.

Having put our gear away for over three weeks, and having only one week to prepare, I had reservations. But this group of fine young men had exerted so much effort, and were so excited when they heard the news, that anything other than acceptance of the NAIA playoff offer would have been unacceptable. We were to play St. Johns, Minnesota, at the Vikings Stadium in Minneapolis. They were ranked at number one in our division. It is what we worked for and talked about all season. Unfortunately, we were still not of championship caliber.

The 1965 playoff game was played in subfreezing temperatures, and Fairmont State was handily defeated — St. Johns 28 and Fairmont State 7. The great St. Johns football team went on to win the 1965 NAIA Championship. Our loss was unpleasant and somewhat embarrassing.

In the end, we had a fine season, but not winning the National Championship was very disappointing — *we got to the table, we did not get any dessert.* The only conclusion is that everyone must work harder.

CHAPTER 5

1967 National Title
Spring and Summer Training

From the perspective of both players and coaches, the 1966 football season at Fairmont State was a disappointment. We had worked hard the previous year, we made the playoffs, and going into the 1966 season we knew we had quality first line players. If we had an Achilles heal in 1966, it was a lack of quality backup players at certain positions.

Comparing the 1966 and 1965 seasons, however, our sense of emergency and our effort in 1966 paled in comparison with that of 1965. The result for 1966 was a disappointing two loses and six wins.

Nevertheless, at Fairmont State that 1966 group of freshmen football players ranks among the deepest and most athletic. One of the reasons for the quality of that group was the fact that for the 1966 season we recruited six quarterbacks; and among high-school athletes, quarterbacks are generally the best because many can be easily converted to other positions such as receivers or defensive backs. Why so many quarterbacks? Simply put, we lost our exceptional quarterback Butch Clayton to graduation, and our major concern was filling the position.

Spring 1967

Approaching our 1967 season, we had fresh memories of making the playoffs in 1965 and then falling short in 1966 — we were hungry. So we approached our 1967 winter and spring training programs with increased enthusiasm. It turned out that both programs were excellent — our 1967 year started with real excitement.

In the spring, just when we started feeling comfortable, a major problem became apparent. In 1966 we had our top two running backs starting on both offense and defense. One of those backs was Larry Blackstone. For 1967, however, we were not deep at the running back position; and we wanted to reduce the possibility of injury. So we decided to play Larry only on offense. But that decision created another problem.

Prior to the 1967 season, Larry and his twin brother Barry had played similar roles — both were defensive regulars who rotated in-and-out on offense. But in 1967, the year that both were seniors, the coaches were asking them to play distinct roles.

After we told Larry that he would only play on offense in 1967, he was greatly disappointed, telling me that he wanted play "both ways." He reminded me that both he and his twin brother had been regulars on both defense and offense for the past two years. I explained the situation, telling him that he was the only experienced running back, and that we had a shortage of running backs — his backup at running back was a freshman who was not yet ready to play full time.

Discussion and Solution

But Larry insisted he could do both; and it was apparent that he was upset because of my decision, and he continued to ask questions:

> He asked, *What would I have to do to play both ways?*
>
> I said, *You would have to be indestructible.*
>
> He asked, *What do you mean?*
>
> I said, *You can't get hurt. If you came out of the game while playing defense and told me that you were injured, I would turn my back and tell you, "You have got to go in and play fullback when we get the ball." You have got to be indestructible, you cannot get hurt.*
>
> He said, *I'll be ready when I come in this fall.*
>
> I replied, *You will be ready for offense.*
>
> He said, *What will I need to do to play both ways that I have not done?*
>
> I asked him, *What are you bench pressing?*
>
> He said, *305 lbs.*
>
> I said, *Make that 600 lbs.*

To me, it was unbelievable that he did not even blink.

> He said, *What else?*

It went on! He gave me a weight (number in pounds) for his curls, I doubled it; he gave me a weight for his dead lift, I doubled it; and so on . . ..

> I said, *If you are playing two positions, you have to do what two men would do.*
>
> He said, *I'll do it.*
>
> I replied, *Remember, if you play both ways, don't tell me you are injured.*

But there were circumstances out of his control. In addition to his twin bother Barry, Larry also had a younger bother. All three brothers were enrolled at Fairmont State and were paying out-of-state tuition. To cover the costs somewhat, all three had small jobs on campus.

Their father leased farmland and harvested hay during the summer. The father, Larry, and his two brothers usually baled hay for about five weeks. The profits helped pay the costs of the boys' education. So when Larry said he would double his present program of weights,

> I said, *There is a problem that you cannot solve.*
>
> He asked, *What is it?*
>
> I said, *You have got to stay on campus and work out under my supervision.*

His home was near Lancaster, Ohio.

> I reminded him, *You have the responsibility of "putting up hay" and you have a commitment to help your father and your brothers.*
>
> He replied, *I will work that out, and I will stay in Fairmont to work out this summer.*

He did stay and so the pressure was on me to try to help him become indestructible.

At that point in time, I reviewed every possibility of where injuries are likely to occur, and how best to strengthen those areas above what we already demanded of our athletes. I reasoned that if Larry devoted his summer to our program, then the least I could do would be to do likewise. (In 1967, the coaches were not paid during the summer.)

Although I challenged Larry to double the pounds on each of his weightlifting exercises, I felt that that mission was impossible. Nevertheless, Larry knew the importance of what had to be accomplished, and I felt that I should devise a program that would help him move substantially toward, if not achieve, his goals.

Making Larry Indestructible

I started with the areas most vulnerable, i.e., the most common injuries occur to the joints: Elbows, wrists, knees, ankles, and neck. A joint becomes stronger when the surrounding muscles that stabilize and protect the joint become stronger; and weights, used properly, can indeed strengthen the targeted muscles.

To learn about weight training, four years earlier we had talked with an Orthopedic Surgeon, Dr. Shen Wang, who helped us with exercises specifically designed for the certain joints. Except for exercising the neck area, Fairmont State had sufficient equipment for the required exercises.

For the neck area, however, we only had a light-weight strap that barely supported 30 lbs. Such a small weight would not be enough to sufficiently strengthen the neck muscles, and none of our sporting-goods outlets had anything better.

Locally, there was McElfresh's Harness Shop, where it was advertised that they had fine leather for bridles and saddles. When I looked at the strap on a saddle, it seemed just right for a neck strap if it could be designed similar to our 30-lb strap. After some discussion, the harness-shop proprietor said he would make one. A week later we had what we needed for the neck exercises. Fortunately, it turned out that the neck exercise program using that newly-designed "machine" proved to be one of the best programs of the summer. With the leather strap, Larry eventually handled 125 lbs. As it turned out, the most important exercise Larry did was building his neck to indestructible. It possibly saved his life.

Summer 1967 Workout Program

Our summer school was made up of two five-week terms. I taught the first five-week term, and then focused on the training for the second five-week term. In addition, *Joe Bundy*, who was our defensive coordinator and was not teaching during the summer, helped with the program both terms.[1]

For the summer of 1967, our training sessions required daily attention. In addition to Larry Blackstone's training sessions, we also trained over 30 freshmen football recruits. On a regular basis, we had responsibilities from 6:30AM until 8:30PM: The freshmen football prospects attended classes 8:00AM–12:00AM and then had training 2:00PM – 4:00PM; Larry trained 4:00PM–6:00PM; and then the freshmen had study hall 6:00PM – 8:00PM. In addition, to reduce the potential for injury to our returning players, Joe would also assist those upperclassmen who were on campus for academic reasons; and on weekends, the out-of-town freshmen had many problems, many questions, and many unusual situations, all of which demanded attention. I felt that it was my responsibility in particular to respond to each and every such situation.

It is impossible to relate all the situations and requests coming from the

[1] I was fortunate to have Joe as an assistant football coach because he was so dedicated to our football program. Joe had played on Fairmont State's 1959 undefeated team, and was a student assistant coach in football in 1964, the year we started our weight training program. Joe's knowledge of weight training, of building speed, and of building endurance was exceptional. In 1967, he was Head Coach of the Track Team at Fairmont State.

group of freshmen that we had in our summer program. Indeed, keeping them happy from 8:00am until 8:00PM was extremely difficult. One of my good friends, however, made a major contribution to solving the entertainment problem. He was Joe Caruncia, a local theater manager, who gave the recruits free passes to the movies on Saturday and Sunday. That was truly a great break for these young men, and it demonstrates that it takes a whole community to get a program to its highest level.

Conditioning Program

Joe Bundy gave his time freely to help serve and support our football players. He enthusiastically volunteered to work with the freshmen, handling most of the duties during weight training — teaching proper techniques and safety when working with heavy barbells.

It is mandatory to have a trained and knowledgeable person supervise new recruits because *without proper supervision serious injury could occur.* Most of our new recruits had no previous training.

In addition to strength training, we also stressed *endurance conditioning* — we had to have more endurance than our opponents because endurance could be the difference between winning and losing, expecially in the fourth quarter of a close game where victory may only be one play away. Again, because Joe Bundy was the Head Track coach, he handled our cardiovascular or running program. We constantly reminded our players of the need for endurance.

If you like to see young men develop their full potential, especially those who have been involved in a rather limited program, then initiate a properly-supervised summer program of conditioning. *A coach will never realize a greater reward .*

As for training programs in 1967, most West Virginia high schools had no more than the basics. Typically, those high schools only had one full-time coach, and if such a coach were lucky, he might have a weight room. More than likely, however, he was working with limited equipment. By 2004, there were a few high schools that had excellent off-season programs, but in 1967, very few had any summer program. And what was worse, many programs had supervisors with rather limited knowledge.

I strongly believe that good coaches will find a way to develop a good conditioning program.

CHAPTER 6

1967 National Title Players and Coaches

As young boys the Blackstone (identical) twins grew up in rural Ohio working on a farm. Farm work in the 1960s embodied the rigors of life — harsh inflexibility and extreme hardship. That experience, however, was their ace of spades when it came to developing into model athletes. I was delighted to recruit an athlete who was raised on a farm.

Hard Work, No Surrender

Folks who work farms start their days around 5:00 AM. If their income depends on their livestock, then every day they must feed, clean, and care for animals. Every day they must be veterinarians — evaluate the health of their livestock and, on occasion, deliver a baby lamb, colt, or calf. If their income depends on crops, then they must work by the seasons, i.e., they must plow fields, plant seeds, apply chemicals, check on water supplies, harvest crops, store crops, take crops to market, design and execute plans of rotating crops, etc.

There is always a need to build or repair fence. They must cut filth — weeds, briars, and other non-desirable foliage. They must maintain their buildings and equipment. And if they intend to increase their income, they will need more buildings — more barns, more storage, or more housing for their livestock.

Farmers face endless tasks, each requiring immediate attention. To survive, they must become accustomed to working under non-relenting pressure. And to be successful, they must develop a work ethic of *no surrender.*

The no-surrender attitude of farmers is historically well documented. For instance, during the founding of our great Nation, it is estimated that more than 95 percent of the "soon to be Americans" were farmers. They worked from dawn to dusk seven days a week; they simply would not quit until they had accomplished their goals. And as history tells us, they did not surrender to the British.

The late Cam Henderson once asked his football squad, *Have you ever seen a fat farmer?* He then promptly answered his own question by saying, *No you haven't, they work too hard.* Placing Cam's sentiments in military terms, the immortal coach Vince Lombardi said it best, *The harder you work the harder it is to surrender.*

My view is similar:

Nothing can make a true farmer surrender.

This "no-surrender attitude of farmers" was perhaps best expressed by Larry Blackstone. In more detail, following the death of his father Dean Blackstone, Larry sent me a letter. From his letter it is clear that Dean served as a model for Larry's no-surrender attitude. In addition, however, Larry sheds light on his father's values — it is no accident that his father's values match those of Vince Lombardi:

First, *God*, Second, *Family*, Third, *Work*.

Arguably, it is those values that undergird the no-surrender attitude. Larry's letter reads as follows except for my use of the italic font:[1]

> ... My father and mother lived and raised their family in Baltimore, Ohio. Dad was in the war at the time Pitti was born, two years later Barry and I, and two years after that Richard. *Dad was a dairy farmer* and with his brother owned probably around 500 acres. Because of farming together, we were as much my uncle and aunt's kids as we were Dad's and Mom's. The two ministers that spoke of Dad at the funeral service, both spoke of his love for community and family. *I think it all started with the farm.* He taught us to share, love, work, show respect and do what was right. He drove a school bus for 28 years and he treated every student the same way. He was on the school board. I remember he felt it was his job to hire the superintendent and the superintendent's job to run the school. He was a farmer, but I think he farmed to provide for his family. Why else would anyone get up at 3:00 AM every morning to milk at 4–6:00, drive a school bus from 7–9:00 AM and again at 3–4:00 PM, milk again at 4–6:00 PM and go to bed at 9:00 PM and do it all over again the next day. The *dairy farm life taught us* all about *responsibility, dependability, and reliability.* The one thing I remember most was that Dad or Mom never allowed our work or chores to interfere with school or sports. We had to work after and before games or practices, but we never missed. I really think as I look back that Dad and Mom were always trying to teach us something about life in everything they did. We visited Dad's mom and dad on Friday nights and Mom's mom and dad on Sunday's. We were close to all of our relatives because that's how they wanted it.

[1]In 1967 Larry Blackstone was NAIA First-Team Defense and Second-Team Offense. He was also the 1967 West Virginia Amateur Athlete of the Year.

> Mom died 21 years ago, but I don't think a day went by that he didn't think of her. He married Bette when he was 70 and again made a commitment that we all watched for the next 14 years. Once again it reminded us of everything that he stood for. When he said something, he meant it. Bette got sick. For the last 7 years of his marriage, he went to a rest home to see her and feed her every day. His word was worth everything to him. *He was respected because he was respectful.* He worked hard and expected all of us to do the same. He was honest, sincere, and dedicated to what he believed in. Mom and Dad were "Special" parents. For some reason, most of what we do and have done in our lives was to please them. We never wanted to disappoint them and always wanted them to be "Proud" of us.
>
> At his showing in the funeral home, nearly 800 people came to show their appreciation for everything he had done. I was really impressed. People that cared for him at the Fairfield village, people that got to know him from Rockmill Rest Home, former school employees, former students, coaches, players from different teams that Barry and I have coached, neighbors, friends, relatives from both sides of the family, and of course family; but most impressive were a lot of parents of not only his children's spouses, but parents of his grand-children's spouses.
>
> Dad lived a good life and a fairly long life. The thing I really wanted to do was call him after his showing and tell him of the different people that showed up. He would have been in Heaven even before he got there. ...

So given my no-surrender trust in true farmers, it should be of no surprise that when I was recruiting football players, I was very interested in those young men who were both football players and true farmers.

The Paradigm of Players

A model for young athletic boys raised on farms is Larry Blackstone — if I had asked Larry to *surrender*, he would have said, *Coach, how do you want me to do that*? In other words, Larry could not understand the meaning of *surrender*. That term was simply not in his vocabulary.

Why do I believe that? Recall that in order to play both on offense and defense during the 1967 football season, Larry had agreed to weight train over the summer of 1967 so that he would become "indestructible." And after 10 weeks of intensive physical activity and training, he was neck pressing 125 lbs. Oh yes, his harness-shop neck strap would have supported more, but he was busy increasing his poundage in all areas of his weight training. I have no doubt that Larry's 1967 summer-of-improvements surpassed those of previous years, when he was tossing 50-pound hay bales every day.

He also improved his speed to 4.6 and his confidence went up immeasurably. Both he and I were ready for our first game of the 1967 season. Although coach Bundy had worked with the freshmen, none of my assistants, i.e., neither Joe Bundy, Bill Kerr, nor Larry Hill knew of Larry Blackstone's exceptional physical development.

First Game of 1967 Season

We opened the 1967 season with an away game against one of our most difficult rivals, West Virginia Tech (WV Tech). Two years earlier, on their field, we eased out a 14-to-13 decision, and we had not wanted to open the season against WV Tech, but as a result of adding a new opponent to our 1967 schedule, we were forced to play Tech first.

It did not take long for Larry Blackstone to reap the rewards of his summer conditioning. On the second or third offensive series, he broke loose for a 40-yard touchdown. Larry's run reminded me of one of (the Triple-Crown-Winner) Secretariat's runs — it looked like the defensive backs who were chasing Larry were choking on his heel dust.

After watching Larry on that play, our line coach Bill Kerr, a coach from the old school who seldom passed out compliments, looked at me and raised his eyebrows. I knew what that expression meant.

At halftime I told Larry that Coach Kerr gave him a nice compliment. Larry, knowing Coach Kerr's demeanor and knowing a compliment from him would be something special, asked, *What did he say?* I said, *He didn't say anything, he raised his eyebrows, and that means 'what a hell of a run.'*

We were successful in our opener to the tune of 42-to-7.

Speaking of Coaches

Speaking of coaches, our 1967 championship team had four: Bill Kerr (Offensive-line Coach), Joe Bundy (Defensive Coordinator), Larry Hill (Student-assistant Coach), and myself.

Coach *Bill Kerr*, with German heritage was also an "old farm boy." He was responsible for the offensive line. He taught the basic blocking techniques for the running and passing games. The skills of offensive-line blocking in the 1960s differ from those of today because in the 1960s offensive linemen could not use their hands.

I relied on Bill's judgments about the readiness of our offensive linemen. If he believed a player could make a particular trap block, then that player could make that trap block.

It was Coach Kerr's philosophy that

> *If a coach tells a football player that he is good, then the coach ruins him as a football player.*

As a coach, Bill Kerr would not pass judgment on a player's ability until he had put the player through the *Briar Patch.* The Briar Patch was a two-step test for an offensive player: To pass the first test, the offensive player must win or hold his own, one-on-one, against a defensive player. And if the offensive player passed the first test, then he would face the second test. To pass the second test, the offensive player must win or hold his own against two defensive players who rush simultaneously.

None of the players liked the Briar Patch until they encountered a similar situation in a game — it was during a game that they realized that it was their work in the Briar Patch that made them successful. But success does not come without cost, and players who endured the Briar-Patch tests always paid the price of total exhaustion.

It is an understatement to say that Coach Kerr believed the linemen's work in the "Briar Patch" should be extreme. His idea was to motivate players to play well in games — players would rather play hard in a game, something they enjoyed, than face the Briar Patch.

Being a perfectionist, Bill Kerr would work all of the linemen with drill after drill after drill. And those who did not want to work hard had an especially hard time. He would make sure that each player mastered the required techniques.

On the lighter side, Coach Kerr also enjoyed a chew of Mail-Pouch Chewing Tobacco — he would get every ounce of goodness from each chew.

His methods? We had a rule for all team members, *If you felt that you should start ahead of another player, you could talk to the head coach.* Then after discussing the player's concern, the coaches would watch the players compete and make the final decision. For an example, we invoked our rule at one point during the 1971 season. We had two highly intelligent and highly competitive young tackles with about the same talent. Each felt that he should be starting. To decide who would be the starting tackle, I asked Bill to make the final decision.

Escorting the two players up the hill toward the Briar Patch, Coach Kerr placed what seemed to be a baseball-size *fresh chew* of tobacco in his mouth. He was prepared.

While the other coaches and players continued with drills, we could hear the moaning and groaning in the Briar Patch. It went on and on. As time passed and we were approaching the end of practice, I told the manager to ask Coach Kerr when he would be ready to join the rest of the team and coordinate team drills. When the manager returned, he said that Coach Kerr needed more time.

Then it started to get dark and we were still waiting on those two offensive linemen. Eventually, we stopped practicing and dismissed the squad. It was only when I was ready to lock up the Field House that they finally appeared.

As they approached, one of the two tackles was walking with Coach Kerr, and although I could not hear everything he was saying, it was clear that the player was pleading his case.

Coach Kerr looked bedraggled and both players looked like they had been dragged through a "briar patch." Then I heard the following:

> The tackle said, *You sure can stand a lot of my pain.*
>
> Taking the now marble-sized chew of tobacco from his mouth,
>
> Coach Kerr replied, *It is the only way to make a sound decision.*

It was clear that the lineman who was pleading his case had lost his bid to be the starting tackle.

Because of Bill Kerr's gift for teaching, I was always certain that when we called for a trap block, it was there. You can be sure of one thing,

> *Those great kids who endured such hard work know what it takes to be successful, they will deliver when they meet life's challenges.*

Turning to *Joe Bundy*, Defensive Coordinator, I met Joe in 1955 when Fairmont State was playing Potomac State College at Keyser, West Virginia. Joe was the starting end on the Potomac State football team, and I was coaching Fairmont. We lost 37-to-7, and even to this day Joe will not let me forget that game. My reply? I remind Joe that Fairmont won the return game 14-to-6.

Joe was in the Marine Corps during 1957–59. Upon returning to West Virginia to finish his education, he enrolled at Fairmont State in January 1959. He played defensive end and then quarterback on our undefeated 1959 WVIAC Championship Team.

As a senior in 1960, Joe had a serious injury and was unable to play. Knowing how he loved football, I invited him to assist us with the coaching, in particular with coaching the freshmen. At that time Joe was 23 years old, and he was excited about such an opportunity.

In 1960 Fairmont again won the WVIAC title, and our freshman team, in a closely fought contest, lost to the West Virginia University freshman team by 14-to-7. By the end of the 1960 season, I believe that Joe was hooked on coaching, and I invited him to an Ohio State football clinic where he met Woody Hayes.

After graduating from Fairmont, Joe was hired at Daytona Beach Senior High School, and then in 1963 he became Head Coach at Clewiston, Florida.

Florida was definitely a football state, and Coach Bundy spent four years in Florida, where he developed an expertise in both conditioning and weight-training programs.

During that time, however, Joe would return home around Christmas, and he and I would occasionally go bird hunting. We would talk, and I told Joe of my experience of visiting the Naval Academy when Roger Staubach was quarterback, and how amazed I was at their training programs — getting the freshmen into school the summer before their first full semester, and having a summer weight-training program that would help prevent injury.[2]

Because of Joe's love of football and his expertise in weight-training and conditioning, I asked Joe if he would join the Fairmont State coaching staff as Fairmont's first-ever Defensive Coordinator. He immediately accepted.

By 1967, there was a no-joke rumor spreading around football circles, namely, *If you are a football coach and you want to develop weight-training and conditioning programs, then visit either the Pittsburgh Steelers, the Cleveland Browns, or Fairmont State.*

The 1965 summer weight-training and conditioning program at Fairmont State contributed immensely to our 1965 football program, which produced an undefeated team. And our mid-1960s summer program (that involved Joe Bundy as one of its leaders) played a key role in Fairmont State winning the 1967 NAIA title.

On the personal side, let me tell you the *Joe did not know Joe story*: The story begins by understanding that Rip Engle, who was at the time Head Football Coach at Penn State, was the guest speaker at one of Fairmont's spring athletic banquets. While Rip and one of his assistants were visiting Fairmont, Joe took our guests out for pizza.

Rip's assistant did not appear to be a football player, and he wore dark- and thick-rimmed glasses. Joe became so interested in listening to Rip tell some of his stories that he turned to Rip's assistant, and then *told him* to go get a couple of soft drinks. The assistant promptly and gracefully accommodated Joe's request. At the time, however, *Joe did not know Joe*, i.e., Rip Engle's assistant was none other than Joe Paterno, the current Head Football Coach at Penn State who is second on the all-time Division I games-won list.

Turning to *Larry Hill*, Student-assistant Coach, I coached Larry as a player at Fairmont State from 1963 through 1966. Larry was born and raised

[2]A summer-school program for incoming freshmen football players is an investment in the student's career. Simply phrased, the demands on a freshman football player are extreme: The freshman football player must not only face his first taste of college life, e.g., the new study routine and the adjustment of being away from home, but in addition, the freshman football player must also deal with the intensity of playing competitive football, which may lead to an injury. Said differently, colleges and universities should provide a *Head Start* program for freshmen football players.

in Fairmont. He played his high-school football in Fairmont, and after two years service in the US Army during the Vietnam War, he returned home in 1963 to become a freshman line-backer at Fairmont State.

Larry Hill, a junior during Joe Bundy's first season (1965), had an interest in becoming a coach. With his desire to be a coach, he not only learned the subtleties of his line-backer position, he also learned those of each position on the defense. His knowledge did not go unnoticed — following his senior season, he was offered a Student-assistant Coaching position for the 1967 season. Larry gladly accepted our offer.

John McKay

Given the title of this chapter, I would be remiss if I did not mention that John McKay also won a national football championship in 1967.

John was another coach with roots in the Fairmont area. He was born in 1923 just outside of the north-east border of Marion County in the town of Everettsville. And from 1934-to-1936 Coach McKay lived in Fairmont. In 1967 he was Head Football Coach at the University of Southern California (USC) when his team won the 1967 NCAA National Football Championship.

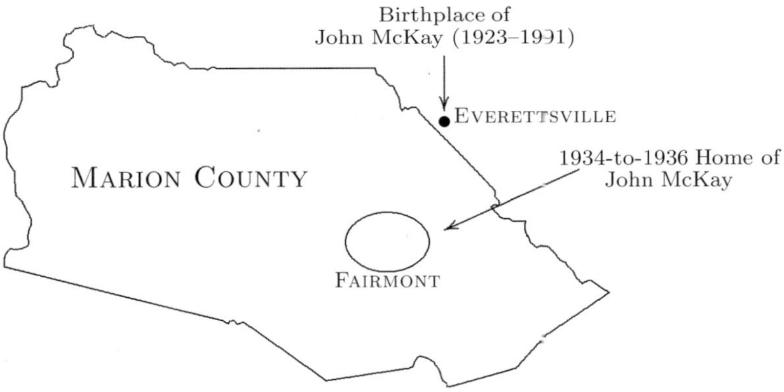

John was a freshman when I was a senior at Fairmont West High School. Both of us played football at Fairmont West. What are the odds that two people from the same high school would become the NAIA and NCAA coaches of the year. In 1967, both John and I were recognized by the Washington, DC, Touchdown Club.[3]

[3]As the guest speaker at a Fairmont State Athletic Department's Spring Banquet, Coach McKay also paid a visit to Colasessano's Pizza: Located at 506 Pennsylvania Avenue in Fairmont, Colasessano's pizza parlor's pepperoni rolls are among the best — Fairmont is known as *the home of the pepperoni roll.* The late owner was "Spider" Colasessano. And as football players and coaches would pass through Colasessano's, Spider would often take pictures and then plaster them all over the walls. I have no doubt that Spider had a picture of John McKay. In fact, Spider and John were teammates on the Fairmont West High School football team.

CHAPTER 7

1967 National Title Regular Season

Following our first game with West Virginia Tech, a game that we won 42-to-7 (see the previous chapter), everything started to fall into place — we defeated Bluefield State 52-to-13 and then West Virginia Wesleyan 48-to-0.

But one of our oldest opponents, Salem College gave us a real scare. We ultimately prevailed 20-to-13, but either school could have easily won that game.

Following the Salem victory, we defeated Glenville 21-to-0 and then West Liberty 20-to-0. So we were undefeated through our first six games.

Buildup to Game Seven of 1967 Season

Our seventh game of the 1967 season was a home game with Waynesburg College. Going into the Fairmont-Waynesburg game, the Waynesburg football team was averaging 60+ points per game. They were undefeated and the 1966 NAIA National Champion. And to make it worse, they were coming off an 80+ point victory over Ohio Northern. They had also been on the cover of *Sports Illustrated*. But the worst of the worse was the fact that Waynesburg was ranked number one in the Nation.

In a scrimmage at home in 1965, Fairmont State had tied Waynesburg, and prior to our 1967 game with Waynesburg, we had moved up a few spots in the national rankings. But we were not one of the top four.

Game Seven of 1967 Season

The 1967 game between Fairmont State and Waynesburg College was played in Fairmont. The home-field advantage was helpful, and we had scouted them as much as they had scouted us.

We had the largest crowd in our school history. The advanced ticket sales told us that we needed a larger stadium. So the game was moved to our county football facility, which accommodates 6000, and then additional bleachers were secured to accommodate another 2000. While these numbers may seem small by large university standards, they were huge for our small NAIA college.

Even though rain played an important role in this game, our defensive schemes conceived by our coach Joe Bundy played an equally important role.

His insights into how to counter Waynesburg's powerful offense was a work of genius. It was a tremendous defensive battle, but we prevailed with a 7-to-0 victory.

The Price of Victory

Following our 1967 victory over Waynesburg, I received, for the first time in my career, several negative calls claiming I had someone water-down the field to slow down Waynesburg's passing game.

In Fairmont, it had rained all day prior to the game and then all day up until the start of the game. Waynesburg College is only 45 miles from Fairmont, and I cannot help but think that during that time it must have also rained in Waynesburg.

Nevertheless, there is no doubt that the rain helped our pass defense, but the calls from the disappointed Waynesburg fans sometimes were very nasty. In fact, there were so many calls, it made me think that those fans had formed a telephone club.

So rather than argue, I reasoned that the radicals were not going to accept the truth, so I began to say, *Yes, we watered the field*! and then I would hang up the receiver.

I later regretted that decision: In 1968, the following year, my daughter enrolled as a freshman at Fairmont State College, and she developed a relationship with another freshman girl from, believe it or not, Waynesburg. And subsequently she was invited to her new friend's home for a weekend. When she came home she was almost in tears — she accused me of watering down the field for the Waynesburg game.

When I told her the truth, she said that she had talked with people who said that I told them I had watered-down the field. It was hard for her to understand why I had said what I said.

Eighth Game of 1967 Season

Our eighth game of the 1967 season was with Central State of Ohio. At the time, an incident on the Kent State campus, which resulted in the death of protesting students, was national news.

Similarly, there had also been violence on the nearby Central State campus, where we would play our eighth game.

Out of concern over the violence on the Central State campus, our administration called a meeting to determine if we should cancel our game. Being undefeated and ranked, however, we needed to play the quality Central State football team because a victory would greatly improve our chances to move up in the rankings. Recall that only the football teams ranked in the top four in the country get invited to the playoffs, and at the time our ranking was hovering around number 10.

We resolved the situation and were permitted to play the game. We arrived on Central's campus to find the stadium closed with heavy security — State Troopers seemed to be everywhere. We were checked and double checked before we could enter the dressing rooms.

There were no fans in the stands, and therefore no fanfare — the atmosphere was a bit frightening. I think it was the first time in my life that I felt apprehensive. But I put on a demeanor of confidence, even though it is doubtful that anyone believed it.

The players dressed in total quiet. It was obvious that they too were apprehensive. But like me, their demeanor was also one of confidence, even though I knew better. In fact, some time after the game was over, a few of our players admitted that they did indeed experience fear.

The press box, located above the stadium, was surprisingly full. Among those in the press box was the head coach of Concord, our next opponent. There is no doubt that he was scouting our team, which helped me focus on the task at hand, which in turn provided a somewhat comforting feeling.

In the stands, however, there were less than 100 spectators. Each spectator had been identified at the gate. There was neither cheering nor emotion, the very backbone of college athletics. The atmosphere was one of serious business and anxiety.

The game was a huge struggle, but we prevailed 8-to-0.

Following our victory, there was neither a celebration nor any "whooping it up." We quickly dressed and left.

Fortunately, there were no incidents and we arrived home safely.

Following the Central State game, we were undefeated with eight wins and no losses. But we still had one more regular-season game, a game with Concord who was also undefeated in the WVIAC.

Last Game of 1967 Season

Since we were undefeated, if we won our last game of the 1967 season we would possibly be ranked among the top four NAIA teams in the Nation, and subsequently be invited to the playoffs.

Our opponent was Concord College. In our 1966 game played at Fairmont, Concord won by the score of 58-to-20, which was only our third loss in the past three years.

To make things worse, we would play Concord on their home field. And although we were favored, home-field advantage is always significant. Again it was a struggle, but we prevailed 23-to-20.

We were undefeated during the 1967 regular season, and we felt confident that in two weeks we would be playing in the national NAIA playoffs.

In the Concord game, Larry Blackstone broke a 30-year rushing record. And in addition to playing every minute of the game, as defensive end and running back, he logged 282 yards and 3 touchdowns in 16 carries. In the end, however, it took a field goal by John Huff, younger brother to the legendary Sam Huff, to win the game.

John Huff, Sam's Younger Brother

It is well known that Sam Huff played for the New York Giants and the Washington Redskins and was inducted into the Pro Football Hall of Fame. John Huff never played much at Fairmont State because he was small at 5'8" and 160 lbs. But John was our full-time extra point and field goal kicker. As a kicker, he tried out with two professional teams, but was not drafted.

Injury Report

We were elated to win the hard-fought Concord game, but we paid a heavy price. Our All-America Nose Guard, Dave Williams, sustained a severe ankle injury. And if we were invited to the playoffs and Dave could not play, then we would be without our defensive leader.

To maximize his rate of recovery, we did everything we could to help mother nature. We immediately elevated his ankle, covered it in ice, and kept him warm to avoid shock. After the game, we contacted the highly respected Physical Trainer at West Virginia University, Whitey Gwynn.

Whitey said that he needed to evaluate Dave as soon as possible. Since we were about 120 miles from West Virginia University, it was 1:00AM Sunday when Whitey evaluated Dave's ankle. After his examination, Trainer Gwynn said, *Dave would be ready to play in the first round of the Championship playoffs*, which would be in two weeks. (Since our victory over Concord left us undefeated for the season, we were almost assured to be ranked among the 1967 top four teams in the NAIA, and thus be in the playoffs.)

Our fine manager and student trainer Pat McGinnis had evidently taken good care of Dave's ankle because he had prevented swelling.

But by Monday, the next day, Dave's ankle was so swollen and discolored that our coaches were concerned about the possibility of a fracture. How could a fracture heal in two weeks? It turned out that Dave's ankle was not fractured, and with treatments every day at West Virginia University we maintained a hopeful attitude that Dave would be ready to play.

Dave's condition, however, made it impossible for him to practice — he could not get his foot into a shoe. So the day before our first playoff game, we were surprised when Dave told us that he was ready to play.

CHAPTER 8

1967 National Title
Home Field in the Playoffs

RANKINGS AND RULES. Following our game with Concord, our last regular-season game, we had to wait to see if we would be ranked among the top four NAIA teams in the nation — the teams that are ranked in the NAIA top four are the teams invited to the playoffs.

When the dust settled and all teams were evaluated by the NAIA ratings committee, Fairmont State did indeed qualify for the playoffs: The rankings were as follows:

1. Eastern Washington
2. Northern Michigan
3. New Mexico Highlands
4. Fairmont State

Being ranked *fourth*, we would play the team ranked *second*, namely Northern Michigan. And since Eastern Washington was ranked *first*, they would play the team ranked *third*, namely New Mexico Highlands. The winners of those two games would then play for the National NAIA Championship.

Since Michigan was ranked higher than Fairmont, Michigan had the option of choosing where the game would be played. At that time of year, late November, the weather in Northern Michigan is typically rainy or snowy. Another factor that had to be considered was the NAIA rule that requires the home team to guarantee, up front, the visiting team a fixed cash pay out and also pay for the visiting team's travel and lodging expenses.

In the end, that pay-the-visiting-team rule together with a concern about the weather enticed Northern Michigan to let Fairmont be the home team, i.e., the game would be played in our area.

As we did when we played Waynesburg during the regular season, we again engaged our county officials who were delighted to host the game.

On game day, the weather wasn't perfect, but the results were — we won 21-to-7. Our dreams of a national championship had taken root.

In passing, we note that the quarterback of that (1967 regular-season undefeated) Northern Michigan University Wildcats team was none

> other than Lloyd Carr, the current Head Football Coach at the University of Michigan. Carr was also the backup quarterback on the 1966 Missouri Tigers' Sugar Bowl Championship team.

As it turned out, in the western NAIA playoffs *top ranked* Eastern Washington defeated *third ranked* New Mexico Highlands. So Fairmont State would face Eastern Washington for the national championship.

Memories of Losing in 1965

No matter the class of the sport, a National Title is something special and we wanted to be special. And as soon as I discovered that the State of Washington typically has 20+ inches of rain in late November and December, I recalled our 1965 playoff game.

In 1965 we had played St. Johns of Minnesota in Minneapolis, and the weather did not allow either team to execute their football schemes the way they had during the regular season.

Indeed, with 10 inches of snow falling shortly before we arrived, we had tried to work out the night before the game. The grounds keepers had plowed the snow off of the field, but it was impossible to have a worthwhile practice.

Looking back, I was the one to blame because I was utterly unprepared for the weather. A smart coach would have studied the local weather projections, would have had appropriate thermal gear, would have had heavier cloaks, would have had heaters, etc. Since I did none of that, we paid for my omission.

On the following day, game day, there was no more snow, but the weather may be described as *bitter cold.* The temperature at game time, 12:00 Noon, was hovering at 17°F, and it dropped to near 12° by 2:00PM.

We were playing on the Minnesota Vikings' field, which is Metropolitan Stadium. It was Saturday, and on Sunday Minnesota would be playing the San Francisco 49ers. So to protect the grass the grounds keepers had placed a tarp over the field. But on our game day, the tarp was frozen to the grass, and it took two hours, with blow torches in hand, to remove the tarp.

In addition, there were unbelievable gusts of wind — at times you had to brace yourself. The chill factor made it 11° below zero.

We lost the game 28-7, but we cannot blame the weather because the wind and cold was on both sides of the field. That playoff-game experience, however, gave me reason to make an agreement with myself. *I will never subject my team to another such situation.* Saying it bluntly, after demanding what I did from the players, and for them to respond without a whimper, I should be shot for putting the 1965 team into an impossible situation. So *in the future, I will do everything in my power to provide our team with a level playing field.*

Who will Play at Home?

Since the NAIA ranked Eastern Washington above Fairmont State, it was Eastern Washington who could decide where to play the Championship Game. If they played the game on their turf, then they would need to raise $20,000.

This time I did my homework. During December in Seattle, Washington, the typical rainfall was 20+ inches. Moreover, they play on a grass field. My thoughts were that instead of playing on that field, with a National Championship as the prize, let's play on a decent field.

Of course Eastern Washington wants the home field advantage, and I cannot blame them. Luck is on our side, however, as a week passes and they cannot guarantee the $20,000 — the home team has the responsibility of paying for any shortfall from their gate receipts, and the team that hosts the game also has the responsibility of paying the traveling and lodging expenses of the visiting team.

As soon as we knew that we were going to play Eastern Washington, the Fairmont State College President, Easton Feaster, called me into his office to suggest that we take a trip to Washington. I immediately reminded him of our 1965 playoff game with St. Johns in Minnesota.

I asked the President, *Could we get the game somewhere in our area?* Both Easton and I did not think that the NAIA would approve our county stadium because it had a limited fan capacity of 6000 — as a member of the NAIA Rating's Committee, I knew our county facilities were not adequate for a National Championship Game.

In thinking about acceptable facilities in our area, I knew that West Virginia University (WVU) was only 15–20 miles from the Fairmont area, and that their stadium would hold 30,000. So I suggested we could play at Mountaineer Field on the campus of WVU. Considering the schedule of activities that are ongoing at Mountaineer Field, however, President Feaster thought that we might have trouble getting the stadium. I had the feeling that he was not too anxious to host the championship game.

Nevertheless, the WVU Athletic Director, Red Brown, was a good friend of mine. So I asked Easton, since I was in his office, if I could use his phone? So as luck would have it, Red Brown was in his office. After checking the dates, Red said that the stadium was indeed available. We have a stadium! But now we need to guarantee Eastern Washington $20,000, and where would we get $20,000?

Easton felt that we would have difficulty raising $20,000 because the weather may reduce attendance. So I suggested that we sell tickets in advance. I told him that I thought our fans would come in spite of the weather, especially since we would be playing for a National Championship.

Easton was not convinced.

> Our President was in his sixth year. I will never forget our first meeting. Prior to Easton becoming the President at Fairmont State, we suffered through about three years with interim presidents, those who could not make too many hard decisions, and we were badly in need of improvements to our facilities, especially the playing field. Simply put, our program was going backwards. At that time we could hardly wait until Fairmont State had a full-time President.
>
> After Easton became that President, everyone wanted everything. So we had to wait our turn. About a year later, Easton called and set up a meeting. I remember asking him, *What caliber of football team would he like to see at Fairmont.* He said, *The best possible.*
>
> I told him that I appreciated his view, and that I would work hard to give him the very best. Then I told him of our needs. I was surprised at how much the President helped us accomplish in one year. For example, the team had to practice and play on the game field. As a result the team literally ran all the soil off the playing surface. When it rained the field looked like a swamp. It needed tons of dirt and ideally a crown. In less than a year it was finished and sodded.
>
> Easton and I did not complete everything, but he worked to help the team with all urgent requests. I surely appreciated the President addressing our needs in a timely manner, and I felt that he truly wanted a quality program. I told my President how much I appreciated what he had done.

So in response to his lack of faith in our ability to sell enough tickets to fund a home game that would be the NAIA National Championship, I reminded him of the tremendous effort those young men had given to get to this point — undefeated and ranked 4th in the Nation. We can show them our appreciation by giving them a true shot at a National Championship. I again almost begged to play the game on a descent field.

But he was convinced we could not come up with $20,000. I will never forget my disappointment. I would have gone to H — for these great kids. Why would my President not support those kids?

I guess the Lord knew how much this meant to my coaches and my warriors. Eastern Washington could not raise $20,000.

So everyone was getting edgy. I was getting calls from our fans and the local news media. Five days went by, but there were no decisions made on the site of the game, and the reluctance by my President to sponsor the national championship game was unchanged.

But Rome was not built in a day.

We seemed to be at an impasse — *I had told my President that if they decided to play in Seattle, or on a less than descent field, I would not make the trip.* Of course that would end my coaching career at Fairmont State.

The number of inquires about "The Game" increased daily. With Game Day just a week away, no one knew what I had told the President concerning my refusal to take the team to Washington. I am sure that if Eastern Washington had raised the $20,000, then the game would have been played on their home field. But they had obviously not been able to raise the $20,000 and our President did not think that we could raise the $20,000 either.

I had numerous student inquiries concerning the game, but at the time I did not realize how great their influence could be. Those great Fairmont State students, students who think anything is possible.

Some 50 students came to my office demanding answers! They wanted to know why no game site had been agreed on and why we could not play in Fairmont. They did not know the stadium in our town was too small to be considered or that we could engage Mountaineer Stadium at WVU. I told them the truth. We can play at Mountaineer Stadium, but the problem is raising $20,000 to bring Washington's team to West Virginia.

> The students said, *We can sell $20,000 worth of tickets.*
>
> My reply, *I have no tickets to give to you, you need to tell that to the President.*

They immediately took off toward the President's Office. Within 20 minutes they were back. The President had told them the school could not permit students to sell tickets. Our conversation continued:

> The students asked, *What do we do now?*
>
> I asked, *How many students were in the hallway outside of the President's office?*
>
> The students replied, *About one-hundred.*
>
> I replied, *Get 200 or more and go back and talk to the President.*

I don't know how many went, but they were successful in reversing the decision and they were issued tickets. In two days they sold $23,000 and before the game they had sold in excess of $30,000.

Thanks to those loyal college kids, we had the funding sufficient to play the Championship Game in Mountaineer Stadium. Those kids had no money, no jobs, and no worries. What they did have, however, was enthusiasm, loyalty, and confidence, which provided Fairmont State with home-field advantage for the 1967 NAIA Championship Game. All that was left was for Eastern Washington to agree to come to West Virginia.

When we contacted Eastern Washington with the news that Fairmont had raised enough money to cover the guarantee, that Fairmont State had secured WVU Stadium, and that the game site was approved by the Executive Secretary of the NAIA, Eastern Washington agreed to come to West Virginia and play for the national championship.

So game day was a week away; both teams could focus on football.

CHAPTER 9

1967 National Title Championship Game

We had a long and hard week of practice in preparation for our Saturday Championship game. During most of our practices we emphasized timing and drills. I had intentionally limited contact so we would be sure to have all of our players as healthy as possible. We were already concerned about our defensive back Marvin Williams, who was recovering from mononucleosis; and our All-American Nose Guard Dave Williams (not related to Marvin) whose ankle was again swollen. Dave's injury occured during the last game of the regular season, and he then managed to play in our first playoff game. We could not afford to lose any of our top 20 athletes.

Following our final practice on Friday, we had scheduled a dinner in the College cafeteria. The cafeteria is only two city blocks from the practice field, and most of the players walked from the field to the cafeteria, but a few had their own cars and would drive.

Larry Blackstone is Injured

One way to drive to our cafeteria was to exit the campus at one of its entrances, go onto a public road (Route 19), drive one block, and then reenter the campus and drive toward the cafeteria.

Our coaches had cars, and on that Friday we made the trip from the field house to the cafeteria. Our "indestructible" running back Larry Blackstone had a 1965 VW "Bug," and he likewise drove to the cafeteria.

When Larry was reentering the campus it happened. Larry's car was hit head on, propelling Larry head first through the windshield. When the police arrived, Larry was bleeding from a head wound. They tried to take him to the hospital, but he told them he had to be at the cafeteria for dinner.

From Larry's perspective, it was great to be alive. From the team's perspective, the star running back has an incision to his forehead and a possible concussion. I am sure that Larry recalled that I had told him that he couldn't get hurt. I had said, *Never tell me you are hurt when you are due to go in on offense.*

So Larry goes to the cafeteria, and is dining with his brother Barry and two other athletes. Likewise, the coaches, without any knowledge of the accident, were also dining at one table of four.

Then two City Police, both a bit excited, came rushing up to our table.

The police said, *How bad was Larry Blackstone hurt in the wreck?*

I Could Not Believe It!

I almost fainted when I turned and looked at Larry.

I asked, *Were you in a wreck?*

He said, *Yes, but I am not hurt.*

I felt that I needed a conference with God. Larry, our top running back in a car wreck with an unknown head injury? Six and one-half months of work and worry? The National Championship on the line? The top-ranked NAIA team in front of our fans? I was numb. I was speechless. I was not sure how badly God hated me.

I had told Larry that if he said he were hurt, then I would turn my back. Larry *said* that he was not hurt.

As the head coach, the only thing I could think of was that I must become an actor. I was going to have to pretend that Larry's loss would not make that much difference in the Championship Game.

Word of Larry's condition had already reached the rest of the squad, and I saw the anxiety in their faces. But I could not bring myself to address the squad. I was a football coach crying without shedding a tear.

As the coach, I had work to do. I had to make sure, as soon as possible, that the players shake the emotional trauma before bedtime. I thought that I had to take Larry to the hospital. But he was nowhere to be seen. Someone said that the two policemen had taken him; I thought that everything was under control.

Later I found out that he did not go to the hospital. (He told me some years later that I took him to the dressing room and gave him two salt pills.) If that happened, I must have had a concussion or maybe we both had concussions. I cannot recall any of my actions or reactions. I only recall my despair. I am sure that I had counted him out as a participant. I recall someone telling me that he had 14 stitches. Larry said that he did not go to the hospital.

I recall my compulsion to address the squad and try to explain our situation and how we would try to resolve it. But I could not or would not see Larry. Unbelievably, I hoped that I would not see him. Not knowing the extent of his injuries, I could not even assume the worst, which left me with neither the courage nor the ability to try to make the best of it.

Even today, I have not yet been able to really seek out all the facts — when I try to recall the events on the morning just before the game, I cannot remember how we got from our campus to Mountaineer Stadium.

I am sure that I was in shock, and I did not recover my composure until the middle of the first quarter when I realized that we were being shutout 14-to-0.

The Championship Game

Larry Blackstone was in uniform. Marvin Williams was also ready. And Dave Williams showed up on game day and told us that he was ready to go. We didn't dare disagree. It turned out that he made one of the key plays. I had already concluded that those three key seniors would be too handicapped to make a significant contribution. Without them, and having to face Eastern Washington, I assumed that we were dead.

To this day I do not know who bandaged our wounded warrior, Larry Blackstone. But he had been cared for. To try to give it our best, I do remember telling our offensive left tackle that he must not permit his opponent or anyone he can reach to tackle Larry.

With our team being shut out 14-to-0, I recall most of the events that significantly impacted the game.

Right before the end of the first half, our quarterback Roy Michael completed a great pass to our fine wide-receiver Jim Mertens. We had scored, and I felt that we were back in the game because we were trailing by only one touchdown.

At half time, I confronted our offensive left tackle Roger Hill,

> I asked, *Why is it that our bread and butter play, the off-tackle running play, is not working?*[1]
>
> Roger replied, *I have never seen or played against a player as good as my opponent.*

Roger's opponent looked to be 6′ 4″ and about 260 lbs.

> I replied, *Roger, there is no more we can do to make you stronger or better. And if you do not improve, you will have me to contend with, and I am tougher than that big tackle from Eastern Washington.*

Roger must have been insulted. On a second-half kickoff, Roger flew down the field headlong into the Washington back who was fielding the ball. The impact was tremendous. Roger not only took the halfback backwards, he dislodged the ball, knocking it backwards about 24 yards toward their goal

[1] Roger was a fine athlete who was the center on a small high school team. He had developed in strength and size, standing 6′ and weighing in at 205 lbs. And since Fairmont State lacked size and athleticism at offensive tackle, we asked him to try the position.

line. The result was that Fairmont State recovered on Eastern Washington's one-yard line. On the very next play, Larry Blackstone scored the tying touchdown *behind Roger Hill's block.*

That play, the big hit on the kickoff, could have been the biggest of Fairmont State's football history. I can remember as vividly as if it were today. But for Roger Hill and his teammates on the offensive line, more was yet to come.

We were playing a great team, and having trouble moving the ball. We finally finished a drive and scored a touchdown to take a 21-to-14 lead.

Eastern Washington, however, did not let us get comfortable. On the next series, they unloaded with a fantastic 50-yard run by their super halfback and tied the score at 21 all.

Going into the fourth quarter, the score was tied.

Our team had worked extremely hard all season, hoping to develop superior endurance. After live practices, we ran 110-yard sprints and then ran 30 stadium steps all out in full gear. We had told our players that if they had superior endurance and found themselves in the fourth quarter of a closely fought game, then they would win.

Our troops were about to test that theory. Would all that pain and dreaded running pay off?

After a couple of exchanges, we started a drive. Every inch gained was difficult, and earned grudgingly. Our student assistant coach, Larry Hill (not related to Roger Hill) was in the press box, and he observed that Eastern Washington's middle linebacker was finally initially-positioning himself far enough away from the line of scrimmage so that we just might be able to block him.

We had a trap play (left formation tackle trap) designed to encourage the middle linebacker to move to his left. And if he took that fake, then he would leave himself vulnerable to a back-side block. Our left tackle, Roger Hill, who had been blocking the huge 260 pound defensive tackle, would get a chance to block a 220-pound linebacker.

Roger, apparently still angry from the half-time incident, was more than ready. We ran the trap play, the linebacker of Eastern Washington took the fake leading to the explosion. Roger Hill flattened the linebacker. To this day, I still enjoy watching and replaying Roger's super block. Our halfback George Edwards ran 30+ yards for the touchdown. At that point in the game, we were now leading 28-to-21 — Coach Kerr's persistence and hard work in the briar patch paid off big time.[2]

There was, however, still 10+ minutes to play. We were worried about

[2]On the "left formation tackle trap" play that George Edwards scored the go-ahead touchdown, not only Roger Hill but the entire offensive line — Jack Reagan, Rich Merrill, Jim Reynolds, and George Shreyer — made textbook blocks.

Eastern Washington's break-away running back. He had already stung us once. But yet again, Coach Bundy made the adjustments necessary to hold Eastern Washington scoreless over the next ten minutes.

It is an understatement to say that Joe Bundy and our entire team of defensive players did a great job: With about two minutes left in the game, Eastern Washington started a drive that looked serious, but Dwight Carpenter, one of our defensive backs, picked off a pass.

Following the interception, we maintained possession for the remainder of the game. Fairmont State won the 1967 NAIA National Football Championship Game by the score of 28-to-21.

CHAPTER 10

1967 National Title Recollections and Reflections

After an evenly fought 1967 football game, Fairmont State College won its first ever National Association of Intercollegiate Athletics (NAIA) National Championship beating Eastern Washington 28-21. In fact, *that* 1967 NAIA *National Football Championship was West Virginia's first National Championship in Football.*[1]

Every player on that 1967 squad deserves credit. They hung together in the face of adversity, survived all challenges, and even in the championship game stepped up when key players were playing injured.

While in this chapter I will mention only a few of the players, keep in mind that the Championship was a *team victory* — without "team effort" on every play Fairmont State would not have been National Champions.

Some of the Seniors

In spite of the injuries that he suffered prior to the Championship Game, Larry Blackstone scored two touchdowns and played an excellent game on defense. And for the 1967 season, Larry was chosen as an NAIA All-American on Defense and Small-College All-American on offense. He was also chosen West Virginia 1967 Amateur Athlete of the year.

Barry Blackstone had an outstanding game and was selected the Most Valuable Player.

Some years later, in 1988, I was attending the National College-Football Annual Meeting in San Diego, California, and wearing a Fairmont State College cap. A young man, who evidently recognized my Fairmont State cap, approached and asked me if I were affiliated with Fairmont State. He said that he had some unpleasant memories playing in West Virginia against Fairmont State. And when I asked him when he played in West Virginia against Fairmont State, he replied, 1967.

He indicated that he was the quarterback (Bill Dedrick) on Eastern Washington's team. I told him that he probably wouldn't like me because I was Fairmont State's Football Coach at that time. Dedrick was a Doug

[1] In 1948, Marshall University had won a National Championship in Basketball. West Virginia University has won more than one national title in Rifle. But no college or university in West Virginia had ever won a National Football Championship before 1967.

Fluty type quarterback — short, but quick, with an exceptional ability to roll out. Dedrick told me that he was currently an assistant coach at a small college. He asked me what happened to that Blackstone who played defensive end? I asked which one? He said, "Are you kidding — were there two of them?" I told him that the Blackstone identical twins played the left and right defensive end positions. His response was, *If I rolled out right the announcer said Blackstone made the tackle, and if I rolled out left they said Blackstone made the tackle. Now I know why I thought "Blackstone" was playing the entire field.*

And how did Dave Williams perform after working with the WVU trainer Whitey Gwynn to rehabilitate his injured ankle? He had an exceptionally strong performance.

I still recall Whitey's *surprising* comments following the Championship Game when he came into our dressing room:

> Whitey asked, *What happened to the Williams boy who I treated everyday?*

I was taken aback because Dave was standing nearby removing his gear. Pointing to Dave,

> I said, *There he is.*
>
> Whitey asked, *Did he play today?*
>
> I said, *You were the one who told me he would be ready today.*
>
> Whitey replied, *Coach, I didn't think he had a chance to play. I told you he could play because I thought that was what you wanted me to say.*

As to Dave's contributions during the Championship game, his play was exceptional. On one particular play, Dave hit the opposing center so hard that the center was injured and taken to the hospital with a concussion. After the Championship game, Dave insisted on visiting the Eastern Washington player. The injured center was very appreciative, praising Dave for his football abilities.

My Feelings

There are certain feelings, perhaps only a very few in a life time, that simply cannot be expressed in words. Nevertheless, let me make a feeble attempt to express how I felt about the coaches, the players, and the managers on that 1967 team: *If ever a team raised a coach, a coach who almost counted them out, none could have done it better than those* 1967 *Fairmont State warriors. They said it with action — not with words.* In short, *We needed each other.*

Philosophy

After winning the 1967 NAIA National Football Championship, the Fairmont State Team was awarded a trip to Miami, Florida to see the 1968 Super Bowl. The game featured the Green Bay Packers and Oakland Raiders.

For the trip to the Super Bowl, we took Frank Lee as our guest: Our local radio station, WMMN, had broadcasted all of our games with play-by-play announcer Frank Lee. Frank and WMMN were among our most loyal supporters, both in good times and bad. So it was only fitting that Frank would be our guest when the football team traveled to the Super Bowl.

As a person, Frank was extremely loyal to his maker. Even on Super-Bowl Sunday Frank attended church and Mass. His story of seeing Vince Lombardi at Mass speaks for itself. From my view, the story *expresses my philosophy* on ordering one's life and is therefore most appropriate for the final comments of this section.

The story goes as follows: When Frank Lee returned from Mass, he was excited. He said to me, *Guess who I saw at Mass this morning*? Answering his own question, he quickly said, *Vince Lombardi.* Continuing, he said, A parishioner came up to Coach Lombardi and asked, *Who's going to win the game today, coach*? Coach Lombardi answered, *I did not come to church to discuss the Green Bay Packers. I came to worship the Lord.*

What made it impressive for me was reading an article in a Sunday-school handout by Bart Starr, the Green Bay Quarterback who starred in that 1968 game.

Bart played on the 1959 Green Bay football team that had only won one-game. That was the season before Coach Lombardi joined the team. Usually, in such a situation, the team cleans house, i.e., many of the players are released, and new players are recruited.

So it was logical for Bart Starr to believe that because the 1959 team had only won one game that he would be one of the players who would be released. But he changed his view after Coach Lombardi's first meeting with the team: Lombardi did not mention Green Bay's miserable record of the previous year, instead he said, *Gentlemen, we are going to have a winning team.* Many of the players who came to that first meeting with Vince Lombardi came with their chin down. But after hearing him speak, they sort of straightened up and became alive — Lombardi said,

> *And to be a winner, we shall only ask that you devote yourself to three things: First, your God; Second, your Family; and Third, the Green Bay Packers.*

It turned out that none of the Green Bay players were released. And the rest is history.

Frank's story shows us how Lombardi himself spoke with actions as well as words. He was devoted to his God, he was devoted to his family, and it is a matter of record that he was devoted to the Green Bay Packers.

Devotion is more than words, it is commitment — *going all out.*

Another witness to Lombardi's 'going all out' was Sam Huff. Sam Huff first played for Vince Lombardi when Lombardi was an assistant coach for the New York Giants. And after Lombardi resigned as Coach of the Packers in 1969, he was hired by the Washington Redskins. One of his first moves was to hire Sam as a player and a Coach. Sam experienced first hand the degree of Lombardi's commitment.

Indeed, as a player Sam had to do all calisthenics that all players were required to do. Sam said Coach Lombardi about killed him doing grass drills. Like hit the ground, get up, run in place, and repeat this until Sam said he thought he was going to have a heart attack.

I see Frank's story about Lombardi being at Mass as an equal commitment to the Lord. He goes *all out*!

Vince Lombardi truly believed that his Maker gives talent to everyone and in return demands that each such gift should not be wasted. Vince's gift was that of helping others to not waste theirs. His record shows that he went all out to make use of his.[2]

[2] As an illustration, let us return to the Vince Lombardi – Bart Starr story. In 1959, Starr, who quarterbacked a team that won only one game, felt that he was not worth much. Starr had lost faith in his ability to be an NFL quarterback, and therefore believed that Lombardi would not want him to return to the Green Bay Packers. But Lombardi recognized Starr's talent, and history shows us that Starr not only had God-given talent, but also fully developed that talent when he was voted the Most Valuable Player in the 1967 Super Bowl.

Like Lombardi, I also believe that *God did not cheat anyone.* Nevertheless, it is my experience that most people have the attitude that they are not worth much. And under estimating themselves, they never develop the talents that they do have. We have to keep in mind that *if we do not give up on ourselves, then God will reward us.*

CHAPTER 11

Winning with Field Position Adjusting to Integration

Football, like most other endeavors, constantly evolves; and if one fails to adapt he will usually pay a price. The truly great coaches are generally ahead of the game, but many become either lazy or indifferent, believing that their success will somehow continue.

After my good fortune to go undefeated (Chapters 1,2,3) in 1952, when we used the Wilkerson Split-T offense, we continued to use the Split-T in 1953 with some success — we won five games and lost two. By 1954, however, using the same offense, we lost five games and won only three. In other words, by 1954 my adversaries had developed defenses that rendered the Split-T ineffective if not obsolete — their defenses had caught up with the Split-T offense: Instead of spreading the defense, the splits between our offensive linemen were being turned against us. Their defensive linemen and linebackers were *shooting the gaps*. They would line up between our offensive linemen, i.e., line up in the *gaps*, and then at the snap of the ball quickly charge through the gap easily stopping or disrupting the play.

1954 Need for Change

Because of our 1954 losing (3-and-5) season I was in somewhat of a panic. I had just finished my third year of coaching at the college level when I began to understand what was necessary for continued success. Looking back, it was in 1954 when I formulated my first rule for continued success:

Keep up-to-date on the latest football schemes and strategies.

In my case, I kept up-to-date in 1954 by attending a coaching clinic. The clinic was organized by Woody Hayes, Head Football Coach at Ohio State and held in Columbus, Ohio. Coach Hayes had invited several well-known major-college football coaches, especially those who had recent success, to give lectures on their theories and to provide demonstrations of the techniques that made their teams great.

Among the speakers were coaching icons such as Bud Wilkinson, Head Coach at Oklahoma who developed the Split-T; Bear Bryant, Head Coach at the University of Alabama and foremost coach of defensive football and its intricacies; Bill Hess, Head Coach at Ohio University who had great success with (in the football vernacular) the *outside-belly offense*; and Bobby Dodd, Head Coach at Georgia Tech who developed the *inside-belly offense.*[1]

I was most impressed by Bobby Dodd's "inside-belly offense" and his philosophy on using "field position."

Field Position and the Inside Belly

Among Bobby Dodd's first statements, I recall him saying,

> We never want to give our opponent the ball unless they are 60 yards or more from our goal line. We feel that they cannot drive 60 yards without a significant mistake — a mistake that will stop their drive.[2]

Coach Dodd went on to say,

> When playing against a team that has a great defense, 60 yards of mistake-free offense is difficult.

Intuitively, the odds that a given offensive series will lead to a score depends on the distance to the goal line. The idea is that offensive teams eventually make significant mistakes. So as the number of plays in an offensive series increases, the likelihood of a significant mistake increases. It was Coach Dodd who went beyond intuition and applied statistics to show that an offense facing a 60-yard drive in order to score would likely make such a mistake and fail to score. Thus, the number "60" became an important number in 1950s football. It turned out that this line of thinking was critical to my game planning during the late 1950s.

Turning to the inside-belly offense, I recall Coach Dodd stressing the importance of having a fullback who was large enough to both absorb the number of hits that he would take and also strong enough to run over defensive players.

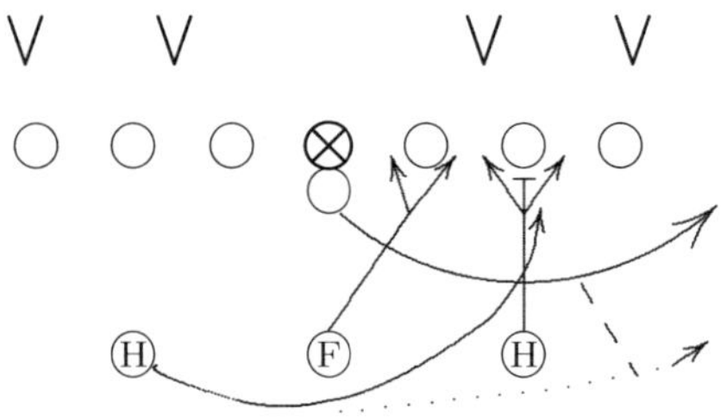

[1]In addition to these coaches, many other successful coaches used the conference forum to explain their football programs.

[2]That was 1955. Today, with many rule changes and offensive schemes that focus on the "big play," many more teams are capable of making 60-yard drives without a mistake.

Before the snap of the ball, the inside-belly offense looks like the Split-T without the splits between the offensive linemen. Immediately after the snap of the ball, the inside-belly offense continues to look like the Split-T, i.e., the quarterback begins by stepping down the line to either hand off or to fake a hand off — *the quarterback does not do a reverse pivot.*[3]

Then, as the fullback is slanting toward the offensive tackle position, the quarterback either hands off (to the fullback), or, places the ball on the fullback's hip only to then withdraw the ball, handing off instead to a trailing halfback who is running outside of the fullback.

The inside-belly offense is dependent on a fullback who can keep the defense busy and worried about stopping him. The quarterback could then fake a hand off to the fullback and give to the halfback, or, fake to both and keep the ball, or, in another step, pitch the ball to the other trailing halfback.

As Coach Dodd said,

> If the fullback, after the quarterback has put the ball on his hip and withdrawn the ball, can continue into the line and be tackled, then the fullback has carried out a great fake and the chances that the play will be successful have increased. The reason is that the fullback has attracted more than one defender, thus there will be fewer defenders at the spot where the ball carrier is trying to run.

Getting Ready for the 1955 Season

I was so impressed that I returned home to install the "inside belly" and to reflect on the "field position" arguments that Coach Dodd had outlined.

For the 1955 season we installed the inside-belly offense and subsequently enjoyed amazing success: We had an $83.33\cdots$ winning percentage over three seasons: In 1955 we won 6 and lost 3; in 1956 we won 7 and lost 1; and in 1957 we went undefeated with 7 wins.

We stressed the fullback's role of making a good fake, and in one of our 1957 games the fullback's fake was too good — an official blew his whistle when the fullback was tackled, stopping the play while our halfback was running down the sidelines with the ball.[4]

---

[3]In contrast, the quarterback who runs the outside-belly offense does a reverse pivot after the snap of the ball.

[4]The play occured during the only game that we lost in 1956, a game between two undefeated teams that decided the Conference Championship. We lost by the score of 20-to-7 and the mishap did not impact the outcome. After the game, that fine official who inadvertently blew his whistle visited me in the locker room saying, *I will no longer officiate any more games.* And unfortunately, he remained true to his word.

The most difficult part of installing this quick hitting offense was that of getting proper timing between the quarterback, the fullback, and the halfbacks:

> *To get the timing right, a coach must adjust the depth of both the fullback and halfback so there is no delay.*

Our fullback was not fast, so I moved him up (lined him up relatively close to the line of scrimmage), and because our halfback was both quick and fast, I moved him back. These adjustments gave the quarterback time to "ride" the fullback and then, if he so desired, make the handoff to the halfback.

At first, it was inside of the huddle that our quarterback would indicate who would ultimately get the ball. Later, as the quarterback became comfortable with the offense, we would let him "read the defense" and choose the best option as the play developed.[5]

In addition to adjusting to our new offensive scheme (the inside belly) in our preparation for our 1955 season, we were also adjusting to *integration.*[6]

Integration in 1955

The first football season that black athletes were permitted to play at Fairmont was the 1955 season. We had eight black prospects that year. Unfortunately, even though our city high school for blacks had some fine athletes, especially football players, none of those players were among the eight trying out at Fairmont State.

In fact, the eight players who were black and trying out for football had no high school experience. Two of the eight had not finished high school and therefore would not have been eligible.

Nevertheless, some of the black players, along with about the same number of white prospects did not respect our team rules — we had a few team and player rules that were very simple and we did our best to explain the rules to all of the players. For example, we had a rule that said *no players would sit on their helmets*, and after several warnings that were ignored, I was forced to dismiss a few players. For another example, we asked all of our players to *run sprints all out to the finish line.* After repeated reminders, however, a couple did not comply and they were subsequently dismissed. We also had other players who broke other rules, and they were also dismissed. By the end of the first week we had to dismiss some of the blacks and several whites. And others, some black and some white, simply quit.

[5]The idea of letting the quarterback "read the defense" and make an "on the fly decision" as to who gets the ball is currently fundamental to many offensive schemes, e.g., consider the offensive scheme used at West Virginia University.

[6]It was 1955 when the West Virginia high-schools and colleges initiated integration.

Because of his busy schedule, our Athletic Director Squibb Wilson was only able to observe our first day of practice — he did not attend any of our workouts until the following Saturday when a scrimmage was scheduled. Arriving at the scrimmage and evidently realizing that there were no black athletes in uniform, Squibb walked over and asked, *Where are the black athletes*?

By not having any blacks on the team Squibb believed that the NAACP would be after my scalp and possibly involve Fairmont State. He went on to express his opinion that I should have given the black athletes more time.

It is possible that he was right, and while I remembered a few of the athletes who were cut from the squad, I was basically unimpressed by those who could not or would not follow the rules. I had moved on to the problems at hand — without assistant coaches and a limited time to prepare, I was absorbed with getting the team ready. I simply could not afford the extra time it takes to continually remind players about simple team rules. So at the end of our conversation, and in reply to Squibb's comments I said, *Squibb, if I am required to keep prospects because of their skin color, not their ability, then Fairmont State can have my job because I cannot be effective under such circumstances.*

Thankfully, there were no complaints.

Integration in 1956

In 1956 Fairmont State had a black athlete who was a fine football prospect. His name? *Moses Guin.* I recall the first time that Moses and I talked:

> Moses said, *May I come out for football*?
>
> I replied, *Certainly.*
>
> Then Moses, in a non-arrogant tone, said, *Last year you had eight black prospects who did not want to play, but I can take anything that you can dish out.*

One of the drills that we used to separate the players from the "want-to-be players" — separate the wheat from the chaff — was open field tackling. During the drill Moses, the only black player on the 1956 squad, was running back punts when he ran into one of our seasoned veterans and an all conference tackle. They met head-on, probably the hardest hit that Moses had ever experienced. But Moses, showing his always-positive attitude, jumped to his feet and said, *Nice tackle*! The veteran lineman, Dickie Laughlin said, *Nice running*!

At that point in time, integration had become acceptable and appreciated on the Fairmont State Football Team. Of course there were doubters, rabble-rousers, and mixed emotions, but all were negated on this team by two great individuals who understood that *performance is the key to being accepted and respected.*[7]

In 1956 it turned out that Moses was the tailback and George Murphy the fullback in our inside belly offense.

Background for 1956 Season

Our first opponent for the 1956 season was Shepherd College, located in Shepherdstown, West Virginia. The game was played in Shepherdstown, and Shepherd had beaten Fairmont State the previous two years by scores 14-to-6 and 26-to-6.

In 1956 Fairmont had neither a spring nor a fall football camp. On the other hand, Shepherd had no spring football, but they did have a fall camp. Relative to our Conference, I would rate Shepherd's coach, Jess Riggleman, as one of the finest, and his 1956 team one of the best.[8]

And since they had won the last time we met by a score of 26-to-6, it

---

[7]To the best of my knowledge, since 1956 no integration problems have existed on the Fairmont State Football team. What I've come to realize is the truly great press and media people we had in that day and age — no one was trying to cause a riff or create trouble of any kind. Arguably, like the game of football itself, some of the drills I used to separate the wheat from the chaff would today be viewed by some members of the press as offensive.

[8]During my playing days at Fairmont (1934–38) we had only one winning season; however, we won two of the four games against Shepherd and tied the other two. Poor as we were, we were slightly better than Shepherd.

was clear that I needed a new strategy. What made the situation worse was the fact that we had only had two weeks of practice, I had no assistant coaches, only a student assistant who was a player from the previous season, and when installing a defense and an offense, it is always easier and quicker to get the defense ready.

It was for those reasons that I felt that we should emphasize defense. And because of the weather at game time, it became more evident that we should emphasize defense. But first, let us travel to the game.

Integration Impacts Travel Arrangements

By the time that we were getting ready to play Shepherd College and avenge the two previous losses, I had realized that Moses Guin was a fine athlete with many talents. He had a great attitude. He had the respect of his peers. And he not only made the team, but as a freshman he was one of four leaders.

We left Fairmont on a Friday evening, planning to stay overnight in Martinsburg, West Virginia. In 1956 Martinsburg was a city whose residents held Southern Traditions.

Our plan was to stay at the Shenandoah Hotel. At the time I did not know that the Shenandoah Hotel did not accept blacks. Being as green as grass, I was not thinking intelligently: When I met the Hotel Manager and he advised me of their "no blacks policy," I expressed my concern about having to have Moses Guin not stay with the team. The Manager said that they had similar problems before, and that there was a black family who could provide a room for Moses. I agreed to his arrangement, but soon regretted the decision — the black family lived five miles from the hotel and thus Moses could not be with his teammates. *How degrading*!

I learned my lesson — *Having been both embarrassed and angered by my fiasco at the hotel, I had decided that if such a situation ever arose again, then I would take a stand.*

Our next stop was the Princess Restaurant for our evening meal where again we were told "no blacks." I immediately told the restaurant manager, *My team will either eat their dinner together, or, if you cannot provide food for all of my players, we will leave and try to find a place that will.*

I just assumed that no one would relent, and that we would end up eating hot dogs and hamburgers on the bus. But the strategy worked: The restaurant manager said he would accommodate us if I would eat with our black athlete at the bar. We did and the next morning we had breakfast at the Princess Restaurant — *we all ate together at the tables.* To the best of my knowledge, Moses Guin was the first black to eat a meal at the Princess Restaurant.

Field Position and First Game in 1956

On our trip to Martinsburg on Friday, there was intermittent rain. And on Saturday, game day, we experienced heavy showers in the morning and then throughout the game. With many puddles of water, the field was a mess.

With only 12 practice sessions before our first game, I was not yet confident of our offense, especially the ball handling, punting, and passing. Knowing that our limited practice on our ball handling skills would most likely be exposed by the weather, my goal was to avoid risking the chance for fumbles.

To reduce the chance for fumbles, I decided to try to keep our opponent at least 50 yards from our goal line — we did not want to beat ourselves. Our punters were good to fair — one was freshman Moses Guin.

Our strategy was (1) punt on first down whenever we were inside our own 30-yard line; (2) run at least one offensive play on first down between our 30 and midfield, and (3) run offensive plays on at least three downs after we crossed midfield into our opponents territory.

To prepare for such a strategy with a muddy, wet, and slippery football, I tried to simulate game conditions during our pre-game warm-up. I had the manager roll the footballs in puddles of mud and water, making the footballs as slippery as possible.

My punter was a great player, but during pre-game drills, he was having problems with the slippery water-soaked footballs, dropping about half of the center's snaps. I asked my punter what he thought, and he said, *We had better let Moses do the punting because Moses is better at catching the ball.*

I recalled that Moses had said that he could take anything that I could dish out. And so far he had. But putting this kind of pressure on a freshman who had never played in a college game? Am I nuts? I asked Moses what he thought of assuming that responsibility and he said that he could handle it. Since we were punting on first or early downs, I reminded him that if he did fumble the ball, then he should not panic and just fall on the ball. We would have another down to get it right. We practiced both possibilities in the pre-game warm-ups.

In the first half of the game, all of our first downs were short of our own 30-yard line. Thus, other than punts, we did not run any offensive plays during the first half, i.e., we punted on every first down.

It paid big dividends. Shepherd was better coached — they ran the ball fairly well and completed a pass or two. Our defense, however, stopped them short of our 40-yard line on all but one occasion, and that occasion occured during the second half.

It is most likely that there have been other instances where one team never ran an offensive play for one-half of a game, but certainly such games are rare. The score at half time was 0-to-0. During the first half, we did not run an offensive play.

In the second half, Shepherd adjusted their tactics — if their first scrimmage play did not produce a gain, they would punt on second or third down.

The game was turning into a punting contest.

Because Shepherd had a fine punter and both teams were exchanging punts, we eventually found ourselves backed up to our 20-yard line.

I always tried to put in one or two wrinkles in every game. For this game my one wrinkle was to fake a punt and run the ball. The reasons that I felt that the time was right for the "wrinkle" was twofold: First, I had noticed that their left end was charging to the inside on his rush to block our punts. And second, we needed to make up the ground that we had lost as a result of punt exchanges.

Seeing "smoke coming out of the nose of Shepherd's left defensive end," I laid a trap for his hard inside charge. I used a fake punt where we would run around his side of the line. Because I did not like to use plays that we had not practiced to perfection, I was fearful about our chances for success — our halfback had to block Shepherd's end to the inside, and the block would be difficult because the end, who was small and fast, would be a rather small and fast-moving target.[9]

If the punt had been blocked, it could have turned out that they would have the ball near our goal line. And I knew that in such a situation we could not have stopped them.

Nevertheless, our senior and experienced halfback did his job! He made a great block that allowed Moses to break into the open for a 40-yard run to our opponent's 40-yard line.

After Moses' run, our guys were ready to play some offense. *But I changed plans.* When they looked to the sidelines, expecting me to signal the offensive play, I moved my leg to indicate a punt. That is, I wanted them to punt on first down. I will never forget my quarterback giving me the double take. He and the team so wanted to run the football. They went into the huddle, and then I assume they all said either coach is crazy or they thought they had the green light. I was frantically kicking my leg in the punting motion.

The players were disappointed, but they lined up in punt formation. Shepherd was more puzzled; they must have figured another trick play. They didn't even put a player back to field the punt. As a result, Moses' punt was perfect — the ball hit the slippery turf and rolled dead at their two-yard line.

On their first play, Shepherd tried to get some running room, but we tackled the ball carrier in the end zone for a safety (2 points). Then they kicked to us from their 20-yard line. We ran the kick back to midfield and

[9] I was breaking my own rule, namely, *a coach should never call a play during a game if the team has not been properly prepared before the game.*

then held decent field position for the remainder of the game. Playing very conservatively, we took no chances and we avoided any mistakes.

So we won our first game of the 1956 season by the score of 2-to-0. The two-year drought was over, but I was saddled with the title *The Coach that quick kicks on first down.*

That was 1956, more than 50 years ago. It is now 2007, and to this day some folks believe we used that system my entire career.[10]

Such a game plan is boring, unimaginative, and not fun to watch or coach. But if I were in that situation now, I would do the same thing, even if no one came to watch.[11]

The goal is to win: *A coach must know the strengths and weaknesses of his team as well as the relative strengths and weaknesses of his opponent. And when your opponent has an advantage in some aspect of the game, then you must design a strategy that counters their advantage.*

Field Position and First Game in 1957

Like the previous season, our first opponent in 1957 was Shepherd College. This time, however, we had home-field advantage. It was a night game; and thanks to our defense we started fast — getting off to a 12-to-0 lead.

The entire first half of the game was dominated by defense; first downs were infrequent and grudgingly yielded.

At halftime our lead had been cut to 12-to-7, and we struggled big time in the second half — we were unable to record a single first down. Shepherd, however, by scoring another touchdown and adding the extra point, took a 14-to-12 lead.

With only three minutes remaining, we had the ball on our own 45-yard line with two time outs. If we had tried three or four plays with no results, then we most likely would not get the ball again — game over. Our best hope was to get field position and try a field goal.

My first inclination was to punt, and *if* Shepherd would not put a halfback back to return the punt, then we just might get good field position. And *if* we could get the ball back, we could then attempt a field goal.[12]

[10]Our fans of the late 50s are now mostly older senior citizens who know otherwise, but a few who remember those years try to remind me of the days when I would have the team *quick kick*. (A punt formation is not a quick-kick formation.) To set the record straight, over my entire career I used the quick kick maybe four times.

[11]Because of the weather, there could not have been more than 25 people at that game, and the majority of those in attendance were blacks. To the best of my knowledge, Moses Guin was the first black athlete to play football in the West Virginia Intercollegiate Athletic Conference (WVIAC), and, two years later, in 1958 when we returned for another game, he was the first black athlete to stay in the Shenandoah Hotel in Martinsburg.

[12]I am sure that at the time most fans would disagree because our field-goal kicker had already missed two extra-point attempts. Some would probably argue that we should

At the time my thinking was as follows:

> Our passing game was not well organized because this was our first game of the season and we had two freshmen backs in the backfield with a fine quarterback who had limited experience in his passing game.
>
> On this particular night, our running game was suspect because we had been unable to get a first down during the entire second half.
>
> I also recalled that in our previous 1956 game against Shepherd when we had bad field position we ran from punt formation — we picked up 40 yards, and that play won that game. Perhaps Shepherd would remember that play and look for a similar trick play, putting no halfback back to field the punt. If that scenario did occur, then we could go all out to force a fumble.

In short, my options were to punt on first down, run on first down, or pass on first down. And the decision had to be made in 15 seconds. Here's your chance to be a coach — *What would you do?*

Well, we lined up to punt on first down. The fans were not sure what was going to happen, but I would guess that they were fully aware of our tactic used in our previous game with Shepherd. I noticed that some of the fans were leaving the stadium, perhaps thinking that a punt would ensure our defeat. But I did not have time to worry about what our fans were thinking.

I did, however, want to know what the Shepherd coach was thinking. And it was most likely that Coach Riggleman was thinking that it was going to be a fake punt because they *did not* put a halfback back to return the punt. So we punted, and the ball rolled to their 8-yard line. So far, our strategy had worked.

But with only three minutes remaining, we could not allow Shepherd to get a first down. We had to force a punt!

To stop Shepherd from getting a first down, we rushed all 11 players: There were two possibilities, first, we hold Shepherd to no gains while preserving time by using our two remaining timeouts, or second, if they had completed a pass then we would have lost by nine points. To me, nine points or two points makes no difference when it comes to losing. So my reasoning was that we had nothing to lose by rushing all 11 players.

I just prayed that they would try to run out the clock by rushing the ball. If we held, then we might get good field position.[13]

I had no doubt that Shepherd's coach had faith in his provenly-successful defense, and (from his view) his best chance to win was to avoid mistakes

---

throw up a Hail Mary, then another, then another, and then another — go for broke.

[13]If we failed, then the Monday-morning quarterbacks would have claimed that our best chance was to pass the ball — anything, but certainly not a punt.

and let the clock run. Whatever the case, Shepherd attempted to play it safe and run for a first down.

We held, and with about 25 seconds left on the clock they went into punt formation. We had an all-out blitz. We did not block their punt, but we did cause a rushed and poor punt, one that resulted in giving us excellent field position.

Aware that our kicker had missed two extra-point attempts, we attempted two passes, both of which were unsuccessful. Then there was no time to waste. With only eight seconds remaining we lined up for a field goal. It was a 38-yard attempt. The kick was oh so close — I was not sure that it was going to be high enough, but then the officials signaled good.

With such a close 15-to-14 victory I felt great; but I did feel some pain for Coach Riggleman — two tough losses, 2-to-0 in 1956 and 15-to-14 in 1957. If you stay in the coaching profession long enough you will have your ups and downs. As Coach Riggleman was leaving the field, he stopped under the goal post and looked up. I knew what he was thinking. I recalled a similar experience:

> In 1961 we were playing West Liberty and leading 14-to-12 with only about 30 seconds remaining on the clock. West Liberty had started a drive and it looked like they could not be stopped. We had dominated up to that point in the game. Then on our 35-yard line they attempted a running play on third and short. Our linebacker was blitzing and stopped the play for no gain. I did not see the flag fall, but our linebacker was called for being offsides. The call provided West Liberty with a first down. Then a pass play put them in field-goal range. The attempt was successful and they won 15-to-14.

Integration in 1958

Integration did not arrive in one day, nor did it work smoothly a year later, or for that matter, many years later. For example, in 1958 I mistakenly thought that the problems that we had experienced with integration and travel arrangements were over. I was wrong!

In 1958 Fairmont State was scheduled to play West Virginia Tech at Montgomery, West Virginia.

Our Athletic Director, Squibb Wilson, was a member of the West Virginia House of Delegates, and he had a good friend, a Delegate from Nicholas County, who owned a hotel conveniently located for an overnight stop on our way to Montgomery. So in 1958 we had planned on staying overnight at Squibb's friend's Hotel.

Nevertheless, knowing that Montgomery was a southern city, and having experienced our previous conflicts surrounding integration, I was worried.

But since it had been two years since we encountered a problem with hotels accepting blacks, I was also a bit shy about asking Squibb to confirm that the hotel in question would accept black athletes.

Consequently, I waited until the Tuesday preceding game day to bring up the subject. When I told Squibb of my concerns, he assured me that there would be no such problem. And when I asked him to call his friend and confirm his convictions, Squibb said that he knew everything would be fine and that a call was not necessary.

By Friday, the day before the game, I was still concerned about our travel arrangements — the team was headed into a largely rural area where there would be no phones and where hotels were few to none. It would be late at night and very cold. Moreover, I was the coaching staff — I had no assistants and I had the responsibility of making sure the players were safe.

So following our 3:00-to-5:00 PM practice on Friday, I once again, almost in tears, approached Squibb, asking him to confirm that the hotel would accept black athletes. And once again, Squibb simply told me that I should not worry, everything would be fine.

So I went to our cafeteria to have our team dinner. Following dinner, we departed for the four-hour trip to the hotel. During the trip I thought about calling ahead, but I had neither the owner's name nor his phone number.

I'll never forget that night because I felt the sting of integration.

We arrived at our hotel after 10 PM. There was a steady drizzle and it was pitch dark. After traveling four hours without a single stop in a worn-out Greyhound Bus, everyone was ready for a stretch — as soon as we stopped most of the squad were up and out of their seats. Hard as it was to do, I told the players to remain seated until I confirmed our reservation.

Curiously, I noticed someone standing in the narrow patio near the front door. Why would anyone be standing outside in cold and rainy weather?

My worst fears were confirmed. I asked, *Are you a friend of Squibb Wilson's and is this your hotel?* He replied, *Yes I am and this is my hotel.* But when I told him that I had five black athletes, he responded that he would be run out of town if he permitted them to stay in his hotel.[14]

So telling the hotel owner that we would try to find a place where we could all stay together, I inquired about directions to another hotel. He replied that he knew of none in the immediate area. It was 10:30 PM, and I had no idea where or when our quest for an integrated hotel would end.

Perhaps we would have to stay on the bus. So we left Gauley Bridge, and drove several miles toward the game site, Montgomery. Montgomery, perhaps the largest town in the area, was the most likely place to have facilities for more than 40 people.

It was 12:30 AM when we found a hotel in Montgomery that would accommodate the whites and find places in black homes for our black athletes. We stayed firm — *I was determined that we would all stay together*!

At 3:30 AM our quest for an integrated hotel came to an end when we found a fine modern hotel about 30 miles from Montgomery. (Even to this day, I am still unable to identify exactly where we were.) Most importantly, it was a place for *all* of our players. I will never forget the owners last name, *Hadad.* He welcomed every member of our party, and we were exceptionally grateful.

Needless to say, the damage had been done as far as the impending game was concerned. West Virginia Tech had the better team. We would have had to play a perfect game to have won. But I am certain we would have done much better under normal conditions. We lost 22-to-0. That shutout was one of only two during my entire 20 years of coaching at Fairmont State.

We were saddened by the loss, but grateful that under the most adverse conditions, Mr. Hadad provided a rainbow. This old coach showed some wisdom, but still had room for improvement. You young coaches take note.

---

[14]In 1956, at the Hotel Shenandoah in Martinsburg, West Virginia, I was confronted with the same situation. I made the wrong decision. Afterwards, I decided that in the future I would not separate team members. And in September 1958, two years later at that same Shenandoah Hotel, I kept the team members together, blacks and whites. I had made a mistake in 1956, and I adjusted my policy accordingly. So having set standards in September 1958, I maintained those standards two months later — in November 1958.

CHAPTER 12

Player Conditioning

It is often said that a coach is only as good as his players. Certainly, there is much truth in that statement. And to the extent that that statement is true, it only makes sense that to be successful, *A coach should do everything he can to make each of his players as good as they can be.* In this chapter we provide the philosophy and some details of the physical training programs that we used in 1967 when Fairmont State won the NAIA National Football Championship. (Conditioning programs have improved tremendously since the 1960s.)

Four Key Physical Attributes

To be successful in football, players must significantly develop the following four physical attributes:

1. Strength
2. Endurance
3. Agility/Quickness
4. Speed

It is well known that to varying degrees, athletes innately possess these physical attributes. It is less well known that every athlete can, with proper training, greatly improve his strength, his endurance, his agility, and his speed.

Commitment Requirement

To maximize an athlete's potential, the coach's commitment to his program and each player must be absolute.

The great coach can motivate almost every young man on his squad. How? By knowing each of his athletes, by understanding every detail concerning the athlete, by having good communications regarding the athlete's concerns, by having good communications regarding the athlete's parents concerns, by showing interest in his progress, by showing patience with his progress, and by showing him love. Such a commitment is a must.

To accomplish the demanding task of helping each player reach his full potential, a coach must be prepared to work seven days a week every week.

The coach must work not only with the less-gifted athlete, but equally hard with the more-gifted, even when the player is a super athlete.

Strength First, Endurance Second

In our training program *strength building was our first priority.* Reaching desirable goals related to strength requires substantial time and effort.

Endurance building was our second priority — a player must be strong for 48 minutes when playing high-school football and 60 minutes in college football.

Simply put, if a coach can get his players to achieve an expected level of strength and endurance, and then get his players in the right positions and have a well-devised offense and defense, a winning season will most certainly be possible. To reach the next level, i.e., go undefeated or win your conference, *quickness*, *speed*, and *agility* are also necessary. While it is possible for a team to reach the championship level with only a strength and endurance program, to stay at such a level requires quickness, speed, and agility.

Second-Tier Players, Philosophy

Coaches should develop all eligible offensive players to be game breakers. Many coaches have a philosophy of letting their best scorers (whether a ball carrier or a receiver) get most of the snaps or passes. Certainly a coach should take advantage of whomever can deliver on game day. But all too often, when the best offensive player is injured, that second-tier player must carry the load.

Moreover, a good defense can cause the best of offensive plans to be rendered ineffective. But whenever a defense applies unusual pressure on a particular aspect of an offense, that defense must be leaving another area vulnerable. Under such a circumstance, the least productive offensive player could be your best weapon.

College coaches may recruit the athlete that they desire, namely, players that fit their offensive scheme. An example is a college coach who emphasizes a passing game. Such a coach may look for more-skilled athletes and a quarterback whose strength is passing. On the other hand, a coach who emphasizes a running game may recruit big strong linemen and good running backs.

A common question for football coaches is the following:

> *What if a coach favors the passing game, but lacks an efficient passer, and does not have the skilled players that are required to implement a passing game?*

A great coach will adapt his strategy to his player's strengths, or he will develop his player's skills to a level that yields team success.

At the high-school level, a coach can get almost anything he desires if he is willing to work exceedingly hard. The key to getting what is desired is *specificity* — research what your desires are, and then initiate the specific techniques and programs that will get the job done.

If speed is the objective, a proper approach to improving speed is necessary. If strength is the objective, a program geared for strength is a must.

Today it is not hard to find a program that targets the development of a specific technique or skill. It is much harder, however, to find someone dedicated to carrying out the responsibilities necessary to run such a time-intensive program. A dedicated coach will initiate the program that he feels is necessary.

Agility and Speed

In 1963 Fairmont State initiated a program to increase agility and speed. The key to speed is *rhythm — if the left arm and right leg are not synchronized and the right arm and left leg likewise, movement will not flow smoothly.* Without rhythm, the muscles begin to work against each other. The result is reduced speed and increased fatigue.

We started our speed program with belts attached to the walls of the Training Room. Then we had our athletes run in place with a focus on rhythm. Both the athlete and the coach could observe when the athlete would fall out of rhythm — the athlete would stop whenever he was working hard but wasting energy going nowhere. We would then analyze the athlete's technique to see what caused his loss of rhythm. *To be most efficient, a runner must have all body parts moving in rhythm.*

When the athlete started to struggle, we would tell him to stop so we could review the cause of his loss of synchronization. Then he would start again, at first running slowly in place so he could be sure to stay in rhythm; then he would gradually speed up until we could monitor the length of time that he could run in place at full speed and in rhythm. Our goal was a time of 10 seconds at full speed without getting out of rhythm. We stressed that the athlete should continue this process until progress occured.

As to other training exercises that improve speed and agility, we used the following three:

Running in place to develop a satisfactory rhythmic style;

Jumping rope to improve agility and coordination; and

Timing the athlete in 40- and 60-yard sprints (after a study of his performance of running with rhythm).

If increased speed is an objective, then the above program should suffice. Philosophically, a coach can get anything that he believes will improve his program, but it takes extremely hard work.

As to the jumping-rope exercise, it will produce results if properly administered. We stressed using just the wrist to turn the rope, not the total arm. We also stressed bouncing on the balls of the feet while not raising the feet any higher than necessary. The idea was to mimic a professional boxer. Our objective was to get as many revolutions as possible in 10 seconds.[1]

We fervently believed in our jumping-rope exercise. So much so that we bought rolls of rope, cut our own Jump Ropes long enough so that the athlete could loop the rope twice around his hands, and provided a rope for everyone. The cost was minimal.

Our endurance exercises included ten 110-yard all-out sprints. The athlete would run the first sprint, and then run the next sprint whenever his heartbeat fell to about 90 beats per minute. And to ensure that the football player would not lose too much of his off-season conditioning, we would also have each player run some 25 steps in our stadium four nights a week (after practice) in practice gear (not in shorts).

Off-Season Training Programs

For off-season training our Defensive Coordinator, Joe Bundy, developed programs that addressed strength, speed, and endurance.

Our *off-season strength workout program* consisted of weight training with appropriate repetitions and poundage. And these muscle-contractive exercises were complemented by their muscle-stretching counterparts. In particular, the weight training for strength was a three-days per week program. We generally worked out on Tuesdays, Thursdays, and Saturdays. There were five basic types of weight training:

Curls

Reverse Curls

Squats

Standing Press

Power Pulls

Each player would be evaluated, and then the numbers of repetitions and sets would be designed to match the needs of the player. In addition, we had

[1] I do not recall the record among all the athletes at the time, but I will always remember the athlete who could turn the rope the most times in 10 seconds. He was a freshman guard standing 5′ 10″ and weighing 230 lbs. He was a magician! What that did for him physically and mentally was unbelievable. He was among, and could have been, the best offensive blocker I was privileged to work with.

a few individual exercises for a few of the players, e.g., the quarterbacks.

Our *off-season speed workout program* consisted of weight training with appropriate repetitions and poundage. And these muscle-contractive exercises were complemented by their muscle-stretching counterparts. In particular, the weight training for speed was a three-days per week program. We generally worked out on Mondays, Wednesdays, and Fridays. There were four basic types of weight training:

Billy Cannons

Jumping Squats

Power Cleans

Bench Press

The Billy Cannons came from the Louisiana State University (LSU) program and were designed to increase speed — the player, with a bar holding 80 to 120 lbs on the back of his neck, would assume a semi-squat position and then move their feet from front to back as fast as they could for a specific time. This would be repeated for four sets. The other exercises are standard, but the repetitions and sets would vary from player to player.

Our *off-season sprint program* was simple. We worked on starts and form. We did leg extensions and relaxation. We had the players competing in 20- and 40-yard sprints, competing not only with each other, but also against the clock.

Our *off-season endurance program* was based on heart-beat rate and repeated all-out sprints of 100- and 110-yards. We stressed form and relaxation. In particular, after a sprint we would measure the heart rate for a period of 10 seconds. We made the following ratings:[2]

30 beats in ten seconds garnered a rating of *perfect*

32 beats in ten seconds garnered a rating of *high*

29 beats in ten seconds garnered a rating of *low*

24 beats in ten seconds garnered a rating of *end of rest*

If a player would measure his heart rate for 10 seconds at 33 or 34 beats, then we felt that he was not in good shape. In such a case, the player

[2]The ratings indicate the lactic-acid build up in the muscles. For example, when the number of beats in ten seconds exceed 30, there is too much lactic-acid, which is not desirable. The idea is to hit 30 beats in ten seconds, which indicates that the muscles are getting plenty of oxygen with no build up of lactic-acid. Then rest and observe just how long it takes your heart rate to reduce down to 24 beats per 10 seconds. *The quicker the better* — the rate of decrease in heart beat serves as a measure of the "football condition" of the athlete.

would rest until his heart beat was reduced to 20 beats in 10 seconds. The receivers could go to eight or ten repetitions, while the "big boys" could do six repetitions. In addition, for endurance we liked to see each player run one mile at least once a week on either Saturday or Sunday.

Our *off-season stretching and flexibility program* was exactly what it says — we set aside time for stretching and flexing.

As Coach Joe Bundy would often say, *If you want to play fast, then you must train your brain and muscles for speed.* That is what we tried to do.

Three-Man Roll

One of our favorite drills for coordination and injury prevention was the 3-*man roll.* It was the drill that we made sure that everyone attempted and understood. It provided variety in the player's workouts, helping them to avoid becoming too complacent and stagnant.

From the mental viewpoint, the 3-man roll provides relief while promoting awareness of possible injury. The idea is that three men, standing about 3-feet apart, start the drill. First, the middle man, say number "1," in a football position with hands on thighs, dives into a prone position at the feet of the man on either side of him, which we may label as number "2." Then "2" dives over "1", then "3" dives over "2", and so on.

The drill has you flat (prone) on the ground, and requires that you get up on your feet as fast and you can, then you go down again, then up again, then down again, etc.

The teaching points are *jump up and over*; *land on your shoulder, breaking your fall with your hands and elbow*; and *rolling over rapidly and quickly, you get to your feet ready to jump over your man.* Learn to roll as you hit the ground so as to evenly distribute your weight and prevent injury.

Many injuries occur in a pileup. It is mandatory that the athlete roll in a game situation. Sometimes the athlete is too exhausted to put any extra effort when the play ends. That is why we emphasized speed and endurance. When the players failed to roll and get up quickly in a scrimmage, we gave them some running drills and reminded them that if they were too tired to roll, then they needed some extra conditioning. They usually responded.

Organizing Training Sessions

At first blush, it may seem that the training programs outlined above were too time intensive. That is, given that each player on the team was involved, there was clearly an organizational problem. To address such concerns let me explain how we organized the training sessions.

The jump rope exercise can be completed in about 10 minutes if you have enough equipment and do the exercise as a group. All players should participate. For the speed training where we have the athlete running in place, we used 10 stations. Be sure the skilled players are in this program. Twenty players can complete this exercise in about 10 minutes. It must be organized. It will pay big time!

Do these Programs Work?

The best measure of the success is the measure of wins and losses before and after the programs are implemented.

Consider that prior to introducing these programs, i.e., during the 1961 through 1963 seasons, our record at Fairmont State was 10 wins 13 losses and 2 ties. I attribute much of that record to our ignorance as to how to improve our program, especially how to implement the training methods described above.

By 1963, however, we had started a limited speed and agility program and upgraded our training program to include a solid strength program with proper instruction, supervision, and dedication. These programs paid big dividends: In 1964, we had an 88.9 winning percentage (eight wins and one loss). And during that year we set a precedent that enabled Fairmont State, over the 1964 through 1971 seasons, to amass a record of 58 wins and 15 losses, i.e., a 79.4 winning percentage. And during those seasons, Fairmont State had one undefeated season; three West Virginia Intercollegiate Athletic Conference (WVIAC) Championship Titles; and one National Association of Intercollegiate Athletics (NAIA) National Football Title.

In short, there may well be modern training programs that are more efficient, but we observed that the programs described above were successful.

The Boy Who Couldn't

My conviction that physical attributes such as speed, strength, agility, and coordination could be greatly enhanced by proper training was reinforced by my experience with the *boy who couldn't.*

The experience involved my wife Florence and one of her girlhood friends. Florence and her friend attended the Methodist Church when they were in junior high and high school. After our marriage, however, my wife joined me and became a Baptist (which proves that anything is possible). That is, my wife had not seen her friend for some time.

And then one day Florence received a call from her high-school friend, asking, *Is it possible to improve agility and speed*? Florence's friend raised the question out of concern for her son. Evidently, the woman's son was a sophomore in high school and tried out for the football team.

Originally the boy had no interest in football, but when his family moved to a city renowned for its high-school football program he became overly interested in playing football. Unfortunately, the coach told the boy's mother that her son would never be a football player because he lacked agility and speed.

Speaking in general terms, I told my wife to tell her friend that anyone can improve if they work at it. After Florence relayed that message, her friend proposed a deal — if I demonstrated a program to make the improvements, she would prepare a steak dinner for us when we came to check out her son's progress.

After some seconds of thoughts, I told Florence's friend that I would do it, if she agreed to tell no one. If I were successful, then the local coach would feel violated, and I would start getting many calls from friends requesting similar favors.

So Florence and I went to visit her friend's family. Based on what I had read, I believed that Chuck Coker's program for developing speed and agility was what this young aspiring football player would need.[3]

It consisted of relatively light weights with more repetitions than the numbers suggested by standard strength programs. Coach Coker had used his program to train his sprinters, hurdlers, jumpers, and vaulters. Using a 25-pound weight during two sets of 25 repetitions, his program consisted of jumping squats; bend over rowing, overhead press, and bench press. All of these were to be done rapidly. The idea was to start the program doing as much as possible while doing it correctly. We included sprints training and as Coach Coker said - always think speed.

The lad did not have a football physique. He was a bit overweight and my analysis was the same as the high-school coach. He didn't appear to be a football player. I doubted that this boy would stick with this most difficult program.

And remembering his parents had showed little interest in physical activities, I assumed I was wasting both my time and the boy's time.

But I underestimated his mother. She insisted on doing the program, and was dressed to try. Saying she wanted to know the whole routine so she could help her son. We reduced the weights so she would not be injured, and she went through the entire workout. She was totally dedicated.

I had been stressing how determined one had to be to really get results, and she obviously listened well. Some weeks later, this determined lady called and was ready with her promised dinner. She was anxious to know if we could see any progress. If the lady had any eligibility left, I would have recruited her.

She took hold of those weights and zipped through the first exercise,

[3]My first attempt at starting a conditioning program for my squad, and before I became familiar with other necessary programs to improve my athletes, was a speed and agility program proposed by Chuck Coker of Occidental College in California.

while her son was satisfactory, but much better than I anticipated. It then appeared to me that the boy would have a chance. This mother had it down and instructed her son properly. And the dinner was Class A!

As time went on, the lad not only stayed with the program that I had suggested, but later worked with the heavy weights to gain strength. As a senior, he was the captain of an undefeated team.

After the season a Football Sports Banquet was organized, and Florence's friend was one of the mothers who planned the event. The mother of the "Boy would couldn't" called to ask if I would be their Guest Speaker.

The football coach who originally said that the boy would not be a football player because of his lack of speed and agility was now the high-school Principal. He was serving as Toastmaster, and he introduced the guest speaker and honorees. Florence's friend had agreed to tell no one of my involvement with her son and she honored her promise.

I was seated next to the ex-football coach (and now Principal) and we discussed the team's trials and tribulations. Since he had told Florence's friend that her son would never be a football player, I was anxious to hear his assessment of this young man who came on to be a regular tackle on the undefeated team.

The young man came up to our table to exchange greetings. And after he left, I asked the Principal how that lad performed during the past season. I knew that was kind of sneaky because this Principal had been a successful football coach and a fine person. In response to my question he replied,

> *I do not know what happened to that boy — he could hardly walk, let alone run, but his coordination improved every year.*

Certainly, one cannot conclude from the success of that one young man (who became an athlete) that the speed and agility program was the sole reason for his eventual success. Nevertheless, that athlete gave the program much credit for getting him to his final goal, and perhaps the program contributed to an increase in his self-confidence which may have played an important role his development.

CHAPTER 13

Time and Tide Wait for no Man[1]

Time and tide wait for no man is a famous saying that means "no one is so powerful that they can stop the march of time."

The phrase speaks to the human experience of the *inevitable*. And like life itself, the phrase applies to anyone in any profession — as soon as one experiences a first day, it is inevitable that there will be a last day. In my case, my first day as Head Football Coach of the Fighting Falcons came in 1952, and my inevitable last day in 1972.

My goal here is to tell the Fighting Falcon's football story during my years that followed 1967, the year that we won our national championship.

1967 — A Dream Realized

After our victory over Eastern Washington in the 1967 NAIA National Football Championship Game, life seemed almost unreal. Everyone associated with the team, especially the players and coaches, had a smile all the time — an exuberance of confidence in a job well done is an understatement.

From the President of Fairmont State, from the Athletic Director, from my colleagues, from the University staff, right on down to every student, there was a sense of unity and group pride that I had never before experienced. It was such a wonderful time. It defies description.

I rank those days following our 1967 championship as among the greatest in my life — my wife Florence and our two daughters Lynn and Susan were so proud of their father, we shared so much joy and heart-felt love.

After the Championship Game the entire team was a guest at Super Bowl II — Green Bay and Oakland in the Orange Bowl. I attended the Washington Touchdown Club on Saturday night prior to the Super Bowl, and flew to Miami for the Super Bowl the next day, arriving just in time for the game.[2]

There were the seemingly never-ending congratulations from colleagues, from friends, and from people whom I had never met. And yes, 1967 was

[1]Evidently the origin of the phrase is uncertain. It seems to predate modern English. The claim is that the earliest known record is from 1225.

[2]The Touchdown Club honored both the 1967 Fairmont Fighting Falcons and the 1967 University of Southern California Trojans, who won the National NCAA Division I Championship. Both John McKay, the coach of the Trojans, and I played football at Fairmont West High School. I was a senior when he was a freshman.

indeed a happy year. Perhaps it will serve as a touchstone for all of the fine young men whom I have had the privilege to coach.

1968 — My Worst Nightmare

On Friday night October 10, 1968, less than a year after our 1967 Championship, I was scouting a high school football game between Monongah and Bridgeport. Nick Saban was the quarterback of Monongah, and Monongah put on a clinic. I have never seen a finer high school football game.

While I was watching the game my wife Florence, who had taught dancing, and our daughter Lynn were conducting a Dance for Florence's Brownie-Scout Troop. Florence had the little-girl scouts make and wear formal gowns — those Brownies looked like "little adults." Our daughter Lynn was a senior Scout and a former Brownie.

On that night, Lynn had a date with one of my freshmen football players, and, along with my wife, asked if they could take our station wagon to the Dance. Not thinking, I suggested that they take our small car, a Simka. I have never been able to forgive myself for that decision.

The Dance was held at the Eagles Club, located on First Street in Fairmont. First Street is just two blocks off of Fairmont Avenue, which runs through downtown Fairmont.

After the Dance, they drove the two blocks to the Stop Light at Fairmont Avenue. The light was green, and my wife proceeded to enter Fairmont Avenue. At that instant, one of four intoxicated young men was driving a heavy car at 85 miles an hour down the Avenue, ran the red light, and hit the small Simka broadside. The football player, Mike Argabrite, survived but my wife and daughter died instantly.

Without question, 1968 was by far the worst year of my life.

Losing my wife Florence and our daughter Lynn is something that has affected me every day since. But having another 19-year old daughter, Susan, I could not and would not quit living — Susan needed me more than ever.

Trying to Move On

At such a time, many things enter your mind. Some evil. And I had some thoughts that I am now glad that I did not pursue. Otherwise, I would not have been able to be with my daughter Susan.

She was a junior at Marietta College in Ohio. And thanks to a great neighbor, Dr. Ormond Haynes, who also had a daughter attending Marietta College, Susan and I could be together — Ormond would bring Susan home on those weekends when I was unable to get away from my work. Moreover, my church family, helping me in anyway that they could, made a big difference.

Each day was difficult. Each night I dreaded bedtime. I would stay up as late as possible, watching television, reading, and working on football (we were in the middle of the season). I would try anything and everything to get my mind off of the accident. As time moved on, I found myself eating pounds of Hershey buds which at first increased my weight, and eventually led to a serious health problem — my heart beat was over 100 beats per minutes. In layman's terms, my condition was diagnosed as *an out-of-control electrical system.* I followed my doctor's orders — I went on a strict diet and changed my behavior. My health gradually improved.

Following the tragedy, I perhaps unknowingly took some of my frustration out on my students and athletes. But I think I kept my focus on football and teaching. Indeed, I coached $3\frac{1}{2}$ years after losing my wife and daughter:

> In 1968, we were 6 and 2; in 1969, 8 and 1; in 1970, 4 and 6; and in 1971, 7 and 3. In short, from 1968–71 Fairmont had 25 wins and 12 losses, winning the 1969 Conference Title and playing for the 1971 Title in a conference game that we lost 21-to-20.

For the 1968 season, the year of the tragedy, our two losses where by a total of three points — we lost to the University of Wisconsin-Whitewater by two points and to Glenville by one point. And for the three seasons after I lost my wife and daughter, Fairmont football teams had only one losing season.

1969 — Perhaps a Playoff Berth

In 1969 Fairmont State was in contention for an NAIA playoff birth. Our record was eight wins and one loss when Eastern Illinois was scheduled to play Fairmont State. A win for Fairmont could possibly vault us into the playoffs. The game was to be played in Fairmont; but as it turned out, the weather had something to say about the game.

The Eastern Illinois team flew into Pittsburgh, where there was a very heavy snowfall. With no transportation from Pittsburgh to Fairmont our Athletic Director, Squibb Wilson, canceled the game and rescheduled it for the following year.

Prior to the cancelation and in anticipation of the game, however, the student Greek sororities and fraternities had shoveled the snow off the Fairmont State football field. And unfortunately, I was not notified of the cancelation until after our players had departed the stadium where they had just finished their last pre-game practice.

As a result, I received some rather nasty calls from a few of the player's parents and a few fans. They were asking, *Why did you make the squad practice in the snow, but did not want to play in the snow?*

Being somewhat upset, I called Squibb to ask why he did not consult with me before making such a decision. While talking with Squibb, I said,

> *I do not want to cancel any game because of rain or snow unless it is impossible to play — when the stakes are so high, you know that I would put forth any required extra effort. But you are the Athletic Director, and it is ultimately your call.*

1970 — Do we need a new Offensive Scheme?

Our 1970 season was disappointing because we had a record of four wins and six losses. At the end of the season I was beginning to question the possibility of changing our offensive scheme because our offense was not designed to utilize the talents of our players.

Installing the Huston Option — 1971

The tragedy that took half of my personal family probably had a greater affect than I wish to admit. But I believe that I recovered to near normalcy by the beginning of 1971, and I rank my coaching for the 1971 season among my best — *after the* 1970 *losing season, we installed a new system and came within one game of winning the* 1971 WVIAC *Championship.*

For details, consider that going into the 1971 season we did not have the type of athletes that we had previously. Previously, we had big backs who were strong and who could grind out yardage. In contrast, going into the 1971 season we had a good mix of experienced linemen and fine freshmen recruits, a quarterback and backup with above average passing skills, and running backs with above average speed.

At the time I felt that we needed an offense that was centered around the talents of our players. Ironically, Coach Bundy learned that Bobby Bowden, West Virginia University Head Football Coach, was going to install such a system, namely, the *Huston Option* (Huston University Offensive Scheme). But to learn the details and teaching points of the Option, we would need to go to Houston. It was 1971, however, and Fairmont State considered the cost of such a trip excessive.

So I called Coach Bowden, and he told me that he had sent his Offensive Coordinator, Frank Cignetti, to Huston to learn the scheme's subtle details and teaching points. Moreover, he graciously invited me to attend Coach Cignetti's presentation to the West Virginia Football Staff. Cignetti's presentation was on the West Virginia University Campus, which is approximately 15 miles from Fairmont.

Because I had yet to decide whether we would or would not install a new offense, and because at the time both of my assistants were involved in other sports as head coaches, I attended the presentation alone. In hindsight, because it turned out that we did install the Huston Option, it would have been easier on everyone if I had asked my assistant coaches to also attend the presentation.

Frank Cignetti did a great job of explaining the Option's strengths and weaknesses. He also detailed the kinds of players required to run such an offense as well as its technical aspects. As examples, consider that the linemen started with their hands on their knees, and on command they shifted to either a three- or a four-point stance; and that the offense used only two running backs, a wideout, and a split end. He also had most of the blocking adjustments for all known defenses.

I saw the potential because most of Fairmont's personnel fit the system — we had quarterbacks who could pass, excellent receivers, and a fast halfback.

So thanks to Bobby Bowden, his staff, our coaching staff, and many talented athletes including several freshmen, we came within one game of winning the 1971 WVIAC Title — we lost our final Conference game to West Liberty 21-to-20.

1971 Post Season

At the end of the 1971 season, our two assistant coaches had to immerse themselves in their own athletic programs — one was Head Wrestling coach, and the other was Head Track Coach.

Since our football season was over, we had gone through the routine of inspecting, repairing, and storing our football gear. I had put the season to rest and then went to visit my daughter Susan in Connecticut — Susan had just started her career as a teacher.

While in Connecticut I received a phone call from our Athletic Director Squibb Wilson, who said,

> *I was unable to reach you at the time, so I went ahead and agreed to a post-season game with Carson-Newman of Tennessee. You have about a week to get ready.*

Reminding me of what I had said in 1969, Squibb went on to say,

> *You told me that you did not want to cancel any game because of rain or snow unless it was impossible to play.*

And certainly Squibb was right — I did make such a statement in 1969 (see the last paragraph in section "1969 — Perhaps a Playoff Berth"); but it was in the context of Fairmont being in contention for an NAIA playoff berth. Under such circumstances I welcomed a post-season game. While talking with Squibb, I thought to myself,

> *It has been two weeks since our last practice, and you want me to remove the rust, change attitudes, practice, travel, and play a game all within one week? You must be kidding.*

The equipment had been stored, the other coaches were doing their own things, and it seemed to me that all of us, players included, had the "season-is-behind-us" attitude. The idea of playing a game in one week seemed absurd — I did not want to play the game, our season was over.

To compound my feelings, I believed that we were not playing for anything. We had recently lost our Conference Championship by a score of 21-to-20, and that loss had removed all enthusiasm for more football in 1971. Had we won that game, we would have been excited about playing a playoff game the following week.

Nevertheless, Squibb had scheduled the Carson-Newman game, and so Fairmont State had made a commitment and we had only one week to prepare. Almost immediately, everything connected with our resuming practice and finding a place to practice was a disaster.

The weather started our demise. Our practice field was grass, and of course we had cold snowy days to begin practice. One day it was impossible to practice on our field because of the snow and ice.

West Virginia University (WVU) was only 15 miles down the road, and they had Astro-Turf. We contacted their Assistant Athletic Director, who scheduled activities at the WVU facilities. He graciously scheduled us for a 4:00 PM to 5:00 PM workout at Mountaineer Field.

I knew that the Assistant Athletic Director had good intentions, but on the day that we were practicing at WVU, midway through our practice time we heard loud music that seemed to be getting closer to the stadium. It was the West Virginia University Marching Band, more than 200 strong, coming around the street leading up to the stadium and marching into the stadium and onto the football field. At that moment the Band Director, Don Wilcox, saw our team just ahead and sounded his whistle, stopping the WVU Band. I told Don that we had been scheduled from 4:00 to 5:00, and that we were practicing for a post-season Bowl. Don said that he was scheduled from 4:30 to 5:00, but he would be glad to permit us to stay until 5:00.[3]

And before I could explain that we were in his house and we would leave, he directed the band to take seats in the stadium.

It was a cold December day, it was now 4:45, and it was not our facility. We immediately packed our gear and departed, even though we greatly appreciated their professionalism.

We fulfilled our obligation to play Carson-Newman in the Share Bowl in Tennessee, but our performance was unfit for such a fine team. We lost 56-to-3. Unfortunately, I broke my own rule of never blaming the team for a loss, and I could not have been more unjust. I will owe that team an apology on every day for the rest of my life. The team was very good considering the circumstances, and it was me, the Coach, who was the culprit on that day.

[3]The WVU Marching Band was rehearsing for a half-time performance in a Bowl Game.

Spring and Summer of 1972

After the 1971 Christmas holidays, we began our winter conditioning. We lost some key players to graduation, but we had a good nucleus of returning players who were working hard — we had a good winter program and our spring game went well.

We had recruited the best and deepest recruits we had had in eight years. It was May and things seemed to be on track — we had contacted our new recruits, providing specific times and dates for reporting for summer school.

It was early June 1972 when President Feaster called me to schedule a conference. To understand our conversation during the conference, however, one needs to know my view of some technical information:

> Since I had no need to know the contractual details between Fairmont State and various faculty members who were both teaching and coaching, I was not sure of the contractual arrangement between my assistant coaches and Fairmont State. Nevertheless, my view was that for the most part, Fairmont State only hired teachers. For example, if Fairmont State had an open teaching position, and in addition had decided to add an assistant coach in some sport, then a person who could fill the teaching position but also wanted to be an assistant coach would be the person whom they would hire. Said differently, it was possible that a faculty member could be hired with the understanding that they would also be an assistant coach, but if at a later date that person decided to stop coaching and just teach, then that person would not be violating their contract. In such a case, it was unclear what action the Administration could or would take.
>
> In addition, I had heard rumors that some coaches, while not being paid directly for their coaching duties, had either received a pay raise or a reduced teaching load because they were devoting so much time to their coaching duties.

With this information in mind, let us return to my conference with President Feaster. Going in, I did not know what the President wished to talk about. He started by saying,

> *I will be candid.*

Then he stated,

> *Joe Bundy has rendered his resignation as Defensive Coordinator, but he will continue as a teacher and Head Track Coach.*

I was shocked and immediately asked

> *What happened? Why did he resign?*

The President did not answer my questions. So I told the President,

> *No one including team members worked harder than Coach Bundy. His attention to detail and his intelligent diagnosis and enthusiasm revealed all of the attributes required to become a fine coach.*

Continuing, and not knowing the reasons for Coach Bundy's resignation, I then said,

> *I guess that Coach Bundy had his reasons, and I respect that.*

Then President Feaster and I discussed several solutions. First, however, he said,

> *We cannot get a replacement.*

He then went on, suggesting,

> *In previous years you were Head Coach with only one assistant and you also coached the defense. You could do that again.*

It seemed logical, however, that because we were losing one coach, we should be able to hire (or recruit from our current faculty) a replacement. So I countered President Feaster's statement by saying,

> *There is a member of the English Department who was a former high-school coach in Pennsylvania, and he has asked me about assisting as a football coach. And there is a member of the Education Department who was a fine former high-school coach.*

President Feaster replied,

> *It would reduce the efficiency of the English and Education Departments if those individuals would become coaches. There are just not enough hours in a day.*

Continuing our discussion, I then said,

> *For seven years I coached with no assistants, but times have changed — it is now very difficult for a Head Coach to compete when he has only two assistants and one student assistant.*

President Feaster replied,

> *Financially, it is impossible to pay another faculty member to serve as coach.*

It was hard to understand why we could not find a solution. And I did not wish to have an ordinary program after working so hard to have a good program. At that point in our conversation I realized that I was not the fair-haired Prince. And thus I was convinced that I must turn the Fairmont State Football Program over to a new director.[4]

So I said,

> *I cannot do justice to the program if I do not have two assistants and one student assistant.*

Graciously, President Feaster said,

> *Why don't you think about it for a few days, and then let me know of your decision?*[5]

I then followed his statement by saying,

> *You are the President, if you do not accept my resignation as coach, then I have no choice but to do as you direct. In other words, if you, Dr. Feaster, say I* must *coach, I will do that.*

In my case, although there were rumors that I had no choice but to resign, those rumors were not true. It was when President Feaster made it clear that he could *neither hire a person as an assistant coach, nor afford a faculty member who was already under contract* that I reevaluated my situation.

To me, 30 years of football, 54 years of age, a health problem, the personal tragedy of losing my wife and daughter, plus reducing a fine football staff seemed more than I could handle.

After 38 years of living athletics and especially football it was a hard decision to make. But the right decision was made. Our fine Offensive Line

[4] I have always felt that I was capable enough to find another job or position. If I felt stressed or uncomfortable or appeared to not fit, then I should look for a new environment. I have seen people placed in positions that were obviously foreign, making them unhappy and unproductive. Such conditions often serve to have a negative affect on their families, but they continue to oppose any thoughts of resigning. Such a situation bruises one's ego, but to resist only induces more pain. Simply put, I refused to get into such a situation.

[5] Was there more here than was being said? I felt that it was not simply a matter of my stepping down as Head Coach. I thought — What will be the consequences if I decided to step down as Coach? Would I face the possibility of also losing my teaching position at Fairmont State, or would I continue as a teacher?

Coach, Coach Bill Kerr, was appointed Head Football Coach at Fairmont State. Our football program ended up in good hands.

Humbling Honors

Looking back, I was lucky to have had the privilege to work with so many fine young football players. In some small way I hope that their experience as a member of a team, where the goals are higher than self, contributed to their success in life.

And I was also lucky to have had assistant coaches who were dedicated to our program and who gave untold hours of their lives to help and guide so many fine young football players.

As a result of our collective effort, I was honored in 1978 and 1988 with induction into, respectively, the West Virginia Football Hall of Fame and the NAIA National Football Hall of Fame.

The 1988 NAIA Hall of Fame induction was held in San Diego California in conjunction with the College Football Awards Banquet, where Coach Joe Paterno was awarded Division I Coach of the Year. At that time I had recovered from angioplasty surgery and the trip to California was a real break for me. My wife Joan joined me on the trip, and we had a great time. The 1978 induction into the West Virginia Hall of Fame was held in the Mountainlair at West Virginia University. To describe feelings at those events, I recall that

> *One feels very humble receiving such honors because of the really great coaches and players already enshrined.*

. . . Deacon Duvall

Editor's Postscript[1]

Early Nurturing. Harold's grandparents, Richard and Laura Duvall, lived on a farm near Fairmont. The Duvall's farm included some of the surrounding pasture fields, but it was located in a wild and isolated area, the closest neighbor living a few miles down the road. Richard and Laura were almost destitute, i.e., the poorest folks one could imagine.

Nevertheless, they were rich in the basics. They had two good wells, and two or three fresh springs. They raised most of what they needed; canned what they needed to get through winter; and their staple was corn — they raised it, they harvested it, they ground it into meal, and they had "cornbread" every meal.

When Harold was about 6-years old, he and his mother had an extended visit to his grandparents farm. Several of Harold's uncles lived and worked on the farm, and his aunt Edna, a younger sister of Harold's father, "ran the house." Early each morning, Edna would make two huge skillets of corn bread; and because the uncles maintained bee hives, there was always plenty of honey. Another substantial and plentiful food was eggs — along with corn bread, eggs with either bacon or sausage were served every breakfast.

In addition to barn dancing in the winter and baseball in the summer, there were hound dogs — every Friday night and Saturday the men would take the dogs fox hunting. As Deacon recalls, *Those dogs were as skinny as rails, you could count every rib.* He also has a vivid memory of his uncle telling him that the dogs needed to be skinny so they can run foxes all night.

Fox Hunting

During one of his visits to the farm at 9 or 10 years of age, Harold's favorite uncle invited him to go on a fox hunt. It was August in West Virginia, where the nights can be a bit chilly. Harold thought that it would be "neat." Along the way, his uncle stopped by the corn field and picked several "ears of corn." Then they drove to the top of a huge hill and met other "fox hunters." Together, they used readily available wood to build a fire. And after the fire had burned long enough to produce glowing red-hot embers, they placed the corn (still in the husk) in and among the embers so the corn could roast. Coach Duvall still recalls thinking that those roasted ears were the best food that he had ever tasted. And at that instant in time, he was a true convert to "fox hunting."

After the feast, everyone found a comfortable place to sit down and listen as the dogs pursued the fox. One hunter would say, "That Ole Red is leading the pack." It was like each hunter could single out the bark of his own dog. To Harold, however, all of the barking dogs sounded the same.

[1] This Postscript begins where Page 2 ended and covers the period 1917–1952 prior to Coach Duvall taking his first college-level coaching position.

Harold enjoyed himself until it turned dark and a bit cool with the dogs barking in the background — at times it sounded as if they were coming toward him, and then they would go in another direction until he could barely hear the barking.

Harold asked his uncle, *How long will it take for the dogs to catch the fox*? His uncle replied, *They never catch the fox, they just run it*! Harold was crushed. He so wanted to see that fox.

That's when Harold ruined his uncle's fox hunt — being the boy that he was, Harold simply wanted to go home, and his uncle gave up his "fox run" so he could take the boy home.

Edna Marries and Goes to Elkhorn

After her mother died, Edna was the woman of the house. She was living on a relatively isolated 40-acre farm and caring for her father and her brothers. The area surrounding the West Virginia farm during the early 1920s had mostly dirt roads with deep wagon-wheel ruts. The mode of transportation was mostly wagons pulled by horses, and one could go for months without seeing a neighbor.

Although she was living in a relatively isolated area, Edna continued to dream of someday meeting someone special and starting her own family.

In contrast to Edna's local environment, Chicago was a city of paved streets, street lights, automobiles, and many people moving to and frow. And in 1923 Harold's Aunt Edna received a catalog with a stranger's name, *Charles Madous*, and his *Chicago* address on the front cover.

For whatever reason, Edna decided to send a letter to Charles, which initiated a mutually-friendly letter-writing relationship. Over time their friendship grew, and Charles wrote and told Edna that he would come to visit her in West Virginia.

Edna's father and brothers ridiculed her, telling her that no one from Chicago would even think of visiting West Virginia. Her family made it more than clear that her chances of ever getting married were slim to none, especially to a man from Chicago.

Later, however, Edna's father died and her brothers moved out of the farm house. What would become of Edna?

Perhaps it was a divine act of the Almighty. Guess who came to dinner? Yes, it was Charles. Charles did come to West Virginia, and eventually he and Edna were married.

Charles was of German decent, and he was working in Chicago. His family members were dairy farmers in Wisconsin, where he had bought an 80 acre farm. Unfortunately, his family did not approve of his marriage outside the German race, and as a result they disowned him, neither visiting nor associating with Charles after his marriage to Edna.

In spite of his family differences, things were going well for Edna and Charles until 1929, the first year of the Great Depression (1929–1939).[2]

Trip to Elkhorn

The year 1929 was not only bad for the economy, but worse for Edna, who developed a growth and had to have major surgery. Her surgery ended any hope for children, so Edna and Charles were on their own.

As a result of the surgery, Edna was not physically able to help Charles operate their dairy farm, whose livestock — 20 milk cows, 4 horses, a herd of sheep, hogs, and chickens — needed daily attention. So in an effort to help his younger sister over the summer of 1930, Harold's father Frank sent Harold, a budding teenager of 13, to work on the dairy farm.

In May 1930, on the day after Harold's school ended, Frank drove Little Deacon from Fairmont, West Virginia, to Connellsville, Pennsylvania. At Connellsville, Harold boarded a train for the trip to Chicago. At Chicago, Edna and her friend met Harold and then drove another 100 miles north to the dairy farm in Elkhorn, Wisconsin. Even today, Deacon remembers how he struggled to stay awake when he was alone on his 500-mile train trek.

And speaking of the dairy farm, Coach Duvall says, *It was there that I was introduced to the world of manhood.*

In contrast, Harold had spent most of his previous summers at his mother's home place, a large farm in Marion County. Today, describing himself when he worked on the Marion-County farm Deacon will tell you, *I was most likely a nuisance who contributed very little — if I were assigned chores and did not do them properly, no one would pressure me to improve.*

"Old German" Work Ethic

When Harold arrived in Elkhorn, he met Charles, an "old country" German uncle who had no help, who could not afford help, and who had accrued substantial debt in order to obtain and maintain the dairy farm. And what was worse, all of this pressure was compounded by the Great Depression. Simply put, Charles did not have the time to tolerate distractions because he was barely keeping his farming business afloat.

As Deacon recalls, *He taught me how to become a man.* German farmers believe you should be able to do a "man's job" at 12, and Harold was 13.

Harold's first mistake was to ask his uncle to give him another job — evidently Harold told Charles, *My job is making me sick*: Harold was pitching (with a pitchfork) *silage* (corn shucks cut up to feed livestock). The silage

[2]The Great Depression was the economic slump of the U.S. and Europe, which was initiated by the stock market crash in October 1929. It hit bottom by 1932, when one out of every four U.S. workers was unemployed.

is stored in a silo, where it ferments, giving off an unpleasant odor.

At the time of his "making-me-sick" statement to his uncle, Harold was just too young to realize how hard Charles had to work. Certainly, Charles did not have time for such "boy behavior." So in response to Harold's request, Charles grabbed the pitch fork out of Harold's hands, and promptly showed the boy how to work. Needless to say, Harold did not get another job — Charles did not speak to him for two weeks.

After that grabbing-the-pitchfork incident Harold completed every chore that his uncle assigned, never complaining. Little Deacon would over exert himself to do each chore just right, hoping to get his uncle's approval.

Charles had 15 cows to milk, Harold worked himself to exhaustion to milk eight — one more than Charles would milk. It was like that at every task. Little Deacon was competing! He wanted to succeed in every way possible, especially when Charles could compare his own effort with that of Harold's. Receiving neither praise nor reprimand, he had a long summer.

When Harold was leaving the farm, however, his uncle was cordial; but Harold had no desire to return. Nevertheless, he did return and at the end of his second summer, Charles gave him $40.[3]

From those summers of working for Charles, Harold developed a deep and lasting respect for those who are raised on a farm. And after a lifetime of experiences, Deacon is even more certain that *It is the farmers who are the salt of the earth.*

Exposure to Athletics

Harold's first involvement in organized sports came in 1929-30. "Little Deacon" had tried to make his junior high-school basketball team. He did not make the team, but he did not quit. And true to his outlook on life, he took the positive view — in January 1930 when he turned 13, the nation heard the first radio broadcast (WXYZ-Detroit) of *The Lone Ranger.*

Deacon tells a story that is symbolic of the Lone Ranger's mask: In the early 1930s, high schools had physical education classes two days a week. The program received little respect from the academic faculty, whose views of "things athletic" were passed on to many students.

In any case, one of Deacon's friends was enrolled in a physical education class for the first time. The teacher told the students to bring gym shoes, a T-shirt, gym shorts or cut-off pants, a towel, soap, and an athletic supporter. As Deacon tells it, "He knew that you wore the athletic supporter to protect your privates; but he mistakenly thought that to get it in place he had to start by placing it over his head — *it looked like the Lone Ranger's mask.*"

[3] In 1931 forty dollars was exceptional: Eggs were 16 cents per dozen and hamburger 11 cents per pound. A postage stamp was 2 cents; a gallon of gasoline 10 cents; tuition at Harvard University $400; and the average yearly income $1,858.

When Harold was 13, in 1930, his family had moved to a location across the street from a City High School. The school had spring football practice and he would watch as the players went through their practice sessions. Being only 13 years old, Harold viewed the players as very large and very strong; and comparing himself to those players, he felt neither large nor strong. He had no desire to play football. But Harold liked and respected the hard-working athletes — if they would ask, he would clean the mud sticking between the cleats on their football shoes. To Harold that was fun.

When Harold was 14, the football world was in shock when a Kansas plane crash on March 31, 1931 took Knute Rochne's life. Rochne was on route to the production of the film *The Spirit of Notre Dame.* The crash dominated the news for some time, and Harold's father gave him a book on Notre Dame Football. Today, Deacon does not remember getting overly excited about the book, but he does recall that he read it. Perhaps unknowingly, Deacon's father had planted a seed.[4]

Over the next few years, Harold's teenage years, he became a reserve on the basketball and football teams, then played second-team varsity basketball, and then, as a senior in 1933 at Fairmont Senior High School, played first-team varsity football and also first-team varsity basketball.

On the world scene in the early 1930s, dark clouds were forming: In 1933 Adolph Hitler took power, and in 1934 he was elected President of Germany.

Back home in West Virginia, however, by 1933 Harold had developed a desire to play football at the college level.

So following Deacon's high-school graduation, he enrolled at Fairmont State. Again, he ascended to the top — Deacon played second-team football and basketball as a freshman, then became a regular on the basketball, football, and tennis teams for three years. By his senior year, he was captain of the varsity basketball team, and second team All Conference in football.

The Cam Henderson Connection

Prior to Deacon attending Fairmont State, Deacon's father Frank was the only member of Deacon's family to attend college. In 1911, Frank graduated from Glenville State College, West Virginia, with a teaching degree. Glenville had three athletic sports — football, basketball and baseball; but Frank had only played some baseball. In fact, until he attended Glenville, Harold's father had seen neither a football nor a basketball game. While at Glenville, Frank grew to know and respect his classmate Cam Henderson.

[4]The legendry Head Football Coach Knute Rochne introduced the "shift" — the backfield would line up in a T formation, then shift into a box formation to the left or right just as the ball was snapped. Coach Rockne had gone so far as to use music as a background to perfect the timing of the shift. Notre Dame used the shift until 1942, when it was discarded by Frank Leahy in favor of the T.

Cam Henderson is nationally famous. The story of his life is well documented in *The Cam Henderson Story, His Life and Times* by Sam Clagg, McClain Printing Company, Parsons, West Virginia, 1981. His coaching is legendary. As one example, consider that Cam Henderson is known in basketball circles as the person who first introduced the *zone defense* and the *fast break*. Briefly, the man-to-man defense was the only defense employed by basketball teams prior to Cam Henderson's innovation:

> Cam's idea for the zone defense emerged from a game where Cam had to coach his team under less than ideal conditions. In particular, his team had to play on a wet and slick basketball floor. Because Cam was worried about his players slipping, he told his players to stay in an area (a *zone*) and guard whomever came into that zone. He then realized that from their zones, the players could break toward the opponents basket in an organized manner, i.e., in a *fast-break* manner.

It is documented in Clagg's book that when the now famous John Wooden (of UCLA fame) coached at Indiania State, Cam Henderson's basketball teams played John's teams three times and Cam's teams won two of the three. Like Deacon's mother Bessie, Cam was born in Joetown, and even today *Deacon's sports hero is Cam Henderson.*

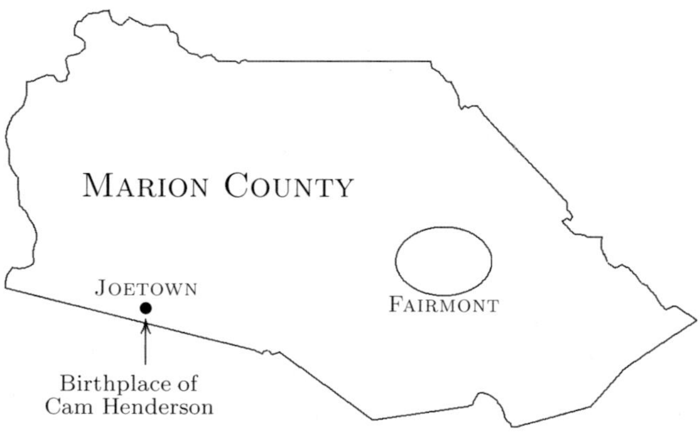

1933 WVU and D&E Football Game

Because Deacon's father Frank and Cam Henderson were friends and former classmates, and, because Cam was the Head Football Coach at Davis & Elkins College, Deacon and his father attended a game between West Virginia University (WVU) and Davis & Elkins (D&E).

Before 16-year-old Harold arrived at the game, he believed that a game between a major university and a very small college was unfair because he expected the WVU players to be larger than the D&E players.

Harold had never seen a Division I football team, and the game was played in the relatively large Mountaineer Stadium at Morgantown, West Virginia. From the beginning, with all of the fans and all of the excitement, he was enthralled by the sheer "bigness" — he could hardly take in all the many activities — bands playing, majorettes dancing, cheerleaders going through their routines, and fans shouting. Those are the things that provide all of the color of a major football program, and Harold was wide eyed and very impressed. What a sight, what an environment! It was great! And Harold wanted to be a part of it.

As the WVU football team ran onto the field, the players were shouting as they would swing their helmets. They were slapping each other on the back as they lined up for the pregame warmup. They looked huge.

The WVU team consisted of about 45 players with several coaches. They were impressive.

Then the D&E team came running onto the field, but in comparison to the WVU players, they appeared rather subdued. The players were all dressed in Crimson-colored uniforms with matching helmets, and Harold noticed how the individual D&E players seemed to look smaller than the individual WVU players. Harold's concern at the beginning was that the group of players and coaches combined seemed so small — there were only 14 in the entire group, which included one coach and one manager!

Harold assumed that he would see the rest of the D&E squad when they started their warm-up drills. But no additional players appeared. When Harold heard a shrill whistle with both teams lined up for the kickoff, he was still waiting for the other D&E players. *Where were they? How can they start the game without the rest of the squad?*

After about five minutes into the game, Harold finally realized that D&E only had 12 players. But surprisingly, the way Cam's boys were playing D&E did not need any extra help — the lone D&E's substitute never entered the game.

West Virginia University scored first. They made a touchdown and added the extra point. The score was 7-to-0.

Then Davis & Elkins went on the offense, using the "Notre-Dame shift." Harold knew that Coach Henderson attended football clinics and workshops, and he also knew that a few colleges, and in particular Notre Dame, used the shift offense.

Throughout the game D&E used the shift, i.e., shifting their backfield just before the snap of the ball, but up until midway through the fourth quarter they had been held to only small gains.

Even at age 16, Harold could see that the shift was causing WVU some problems because one of the WVU players was constantly directing the linemen and helping them to get properly located. Harold also noticed a general confusion on the part of the WVU defense, which was no doubt also due to Coach Cam's shift strategy.

Then D&E had the ball about midfield near the right sideline. In those days the referees did not spot the ball some 15 yards from the sidelines, they just moved the ball enough to allow the offensive team to line up.

Running room was to the left. And Harold, like all the fans in the stadium and the WVU players in particular, were ready for D&E to run to the left. And sure enough, the split formation began moving in that direction — offensive linemen were pulling with a couple of backs close behind and all were moving left. At the beginning of the play, everyone assumed that one of those backs was carrying the ball.

But wait. On the right side of the field near the side line, the fans gradually noticed a D&E player running 10 yards down field with the ball. He was all alone and headed for the end zone. Then he scored. The extra point was successful and the score was 7-to-7.

The game ended in a tie.

For Harold it was a great moment — a small college playing a major university to a draw. Without knowing it, on that day Cam Henderson, Harold's hero, taught Harold a lesson. The lesson was simply that *the belief that winning football teams have larger players and larger squads than their opponents is a myth.*

1934–38 at Fairmont State

What Sport? Following the 1933 WVU and D&E football game, Harold's view of playing football at the college level changed. Before that game Harold was a 16 year-old high-school football player with no desire to play college-level football. After that game Harold was determined to play college-level football.

And play he did! Harold not only played football, he was an all-conference selection at Fairmont State for the 1937 season.

As a freshman in 1934-35, Harold made both the basketball and football traveling squads. But with his height at 5′ 9″ and his weight at about 125 lbs, he was among the smallest of the players. From his view, his relatively small stature made his future in either basketball or football uncertain.

Harold had played one year of baseball in high school, and at that time he felt that baseball might be his sport. His father was a baseball fan, and Harold sensed that his dad wanted him to try baseball. So Harold did try baseball; and he did travel with the baseball team, but he never played.

It was after Harold decided that his future would not include baseball that he was *discovered* by the tennis coach.

The tennis coach attended every basketball game, and after observing Harold's athletic skills first hand and then learning that Harold was no longer playing baseball, the tennis coach asked Harold to try out for tennis.[5]

Harold accepted the offer, but his first year was a struggle. He enjoyed three years of playing tennis but he still feels the pain of so many losses.[6]

In summary, as a student-athlete at Fairmont State Harold played basketball, football, and tennis.

1937 Football Game

It was during his senior year that Deacon most likely learned about the value of having the quarterback communicate the play to his teammates prior to the snap of the ball.

The 1937 Fairmont State football team started the season by trying to run the single-wing offense. After having almost no success, the team turned to the double-wing. But again, the offensive scheme was a failure. The problem was that both the single- and double-wing systems could not be successful without successful running plays, and simply put, that 1937 team could not run the football. So the next step was that of abandoning the focus on the run. The idea was to position the quarterback five yards behind the center prior to the snap of the ball, and then try to complete passes to the wing backs.

In 1937 this formation was called the *short-punt formation*, the name arising from the fact that the quarterback was in position to punt on every down. Today, the formation is well-known as the *shot-gun*.

To run the shot-gun, however, the team needed wing backs who could catch a pass on the run. And because Harold was the only wing back that could catch a pass on the run, his role in the offense was demanding.

Deacon still recalls one game in particular. It was a hot, dry, and dusty day. It was the second half and the score was tied at 0-to-0. He had been in motion on every play, i.e., he lined up at left wing, ran across the formation, went out about five years beyond the right end, turned up field, and then tried to outrun the defensive back. To be sure, Harold was getting tired.

---

[5]As a senior in high school, Harold had been the last, or sixth man on the tennis team. Because of the Great Depression, the Board of Education had dropped all athletics. Nevertheless, a couple of high-school seniors decided to organize a tennis team — the seniors would furnish their own equipment. Since there were three asphalt courts maintained within the City, the team was like a private club that carried the high-school name. Their competition consisted of two other high-school tennis teams and two private-club teams. No one on Harold's team had much experience.

[6]Fairmont State had a tennis team only because the Chairman of the Social Science Department loved tennis and volunteered to coach the team and use his own car to transport the team at no cost to Fairmont State. Fairmont State did, however, maintain the clay courts and furnished the tennis balls.

In those days there was only one salaried coach at Fairmont State, Jasper Colebank. In fact, he was the only member of the Athletic Department, and he was responsible for football, basketball, and baseball.

Then on one play, he went in motion, ran up the field, looked back, and saw a perfect spiral headed in his direction. The ball was going to go over his head, so he tried to change gears to increase his speed. To have a chance at making the catch, he had to dive for the ball.

But the ball was out of Harold's reach. He hit the ground, dust flew, and his momentum carried him face-first into the visitor's bench. He was not seriously injured. He did have dust everywhere, his forearms and elbows were skinned, and his face was stinging from the impact with the bench. Deacon will tell you that he had never seen such a tight spiral or more perfect pass. He was so disappointed — he felt that he should have made that catch.

When Deacon returned to the huddle he apologized to the quarterback. The quarterback replied, *I am glad you didn't touch it. I changed my mind and punted the ball.* Deacon said, *You son-of-a _____. I am wounded because you can't tell me what is going on?* Given the 1937 rules of the game, I have often wondered what the opposing players thought of my intelligence.[7]

1938 Basketball Trip

For the most part, athletes who play on organized sports teams are exposed to strict rules and regulations. In such an environment a young boy may greatly benefit from the advice of his older and wiser coach. Coach Duvall believes that such exposure improves the athlete's character, helping them not only in athletics, but throughout their entire lives.

To illustrate how a coach can remind his players of basic principles, I think that Deacon's story below reflects how Deacon himself, years later, would impart core values to his players.

Deacon's story is presented in his own words. He recalls his senior year 1937-38 at Fairmont State, when the basketball team had a two-game two-night trip from Fairmont to Wheeling by private automobile.

> The Head Coach, Jasper Colebank, used his huge Chrysler to transport one-half of the team, and if Jasper knew that a player whom he trusted had a car, then he would allow that player to transport the other half. The team had no assistant coach, no trainer, no manager, and no sports information director.
>
> Only two players had access to a car, namely, Ned Pence, whose father was Dean of Instruction at Fairmont State, and me. Ned and I alternated taking our cars, and it was my turn.
>
> Coach Colebank's car was leading our two-car caravan, but during the trip we fell behind and lost sight of his car. Coach Colebank and the other players continued toward Wheeling — unaware of exactly where we were.

[7] In 1937, the punting team would be penalized if they touched the ball before the receiving team.

The route to Wheeling passed through the home town of a former teammate, and we decided to stop for a few moments. It had been snowing, but the highways were relatively clear. What we did not know was that to get to our teammate's house we had to walk over one-half mile up a steep incline covered with about six inches of snow.

Had I known about the time and effort necessary to visit our friend, I would not have stopped for the visit. Hardly halfway up the incline, I started worrying that Coach Colebank would be concerned about where we were.

When we arrived at our friend's house, however, he was in the final stages of TB and too weak to carry on an extended conversation. So I was glad that we went to see him because he passed away six weeks later at the age of 21.

When we returned to the car, I expressed my concern about our coach being unhappy with me because we had stopped — I was team captain and, like the other players, had great respect for Coach Colebank. Nevertheless, I was unsure of his reaction to my decision to stop and visit a former teammate.

When we finally arrived in Wheeling, possibly an hour late, I drove up to the front of the hotel and told my teammates to tell Coach Colebank what had happened while I parked the car. One teammate riding in my car did his own rationalizing, trying to spare me the coach's wrath.

When I entered the hotel, the first person to appear was Coach Colebank. He asked, *What kind of car trouble did you have*? Not knowing that a teammate had already given an alibi, I answered, *We did not have car trouble.* And then I told him what had happened. The Coach then confronted the athlete who had given him the alibi and said, *Anyone who will lie will steal, from now on you will not only ride with me, you will sit beside me so I can keep an eye on you.*

(1936–38) Best Job on Campus

Perhaps it is only those who endured the Great Depression who can truly understand the hardships. It was during the late 1930s that the pain was everywhere. Many had lost their jobs earlier and had to struggle. College students, in many cases, had to drop out of school and look for any kind of work. The students at Fairmont State were no exception, and even those who did not drop out of school had to make do on very little.

Harold was fortunate in that his father was a postal employee who had a regular and reliable income that covered the basics. Nevertheless, Harold had to (and did) find summer jobs. If you were a student athlete who needed cash, times were tough.

The Head Football Coach at Fairmont State in 1936 was Jasper Colebank. Jasper asked his players if anyone would want the job of washing/laundering the football equipment — the pants, jerseys, socks, towels, and athletic supporters. The pay was based on the numbers and kinds of equipment that were washed — to wash an athletic supporter, the College would pay five cents, for a jersey, 15 cents, etc. (In those days football players did not wear T-shirts under their shoulder pads.)

After Harold figured out how much he could earn by doing "the team's laundry," he told the coach he would do the entire job. Harold got the job, and during his junior and senior years he provided Fairmont State with clean football gear. (In those years automatic washers and dryers did not exist.)

So as a junior and senior at Fairmont State, Harold did laundry — it wasn't so bad, except for the months of October and November. During that time, the numbers of cloudy and rainy days, along with the snow in late November, made it difficult to find enough space to hang the laundry *out to dry*. With his studies, his four-days per week scrimmages, and his laundry job, he had no trouble going to sleep, and he had cash for a small-scale social life. As Harold says, *I was the wealthiest student on campus.*

1938 Student-Assistant Coach

At the end of his senior 1937 season, the Head Football Coach asked Harold if he would accept the position of Student-Assistant Coach with the Fairmont State 1938 team. Harold accepted. After his first season (1938) as a coach, Coach Duvall graduated from Fairmont State the following semester (1939), and his star was rising.

1939 Deacon meets Florence

During the winter of 1939 Deacon became the basketball coach for the Fairmont Business College. The Business College President, knowing that Deacon had played basketball at Fairmont State, told Deacon that he could take business courses tuition free if he would be willing to coach the Business College's men's basketball team. Deacon accepted and then enrolled in bookkeeping and typing while serving as the Men's Basketball Coach.

The Men's Basketball Team and the Women's Basketball Team played on the same nights on the same courts. By chance, there was a lovely young woman, *Florence Vaughan*, who was on the Women's Team.[8]

Love blossomed — Deacon and Florence were married in August 1941.

[8]Florence was born in Fairmont, and had been a Princess in the Forest Festival in Elkins, West Virginia. Her father was a General Foreman at the Baltimore and Ohio (B&O) Roundhouse in Fairmont. Deacon's wife Florence worked until their two daughters, Lynn and Susan, were born.

1941–42 Coaching at Barrackville

Following his graduation from Fairmont State in 1939, Deacon enrolled in Columbia University in August of 1940. But after one semester of graduate studies, Deacon was offered a teaching and coaching position in Barrackville, which is located in Marion County.[9]

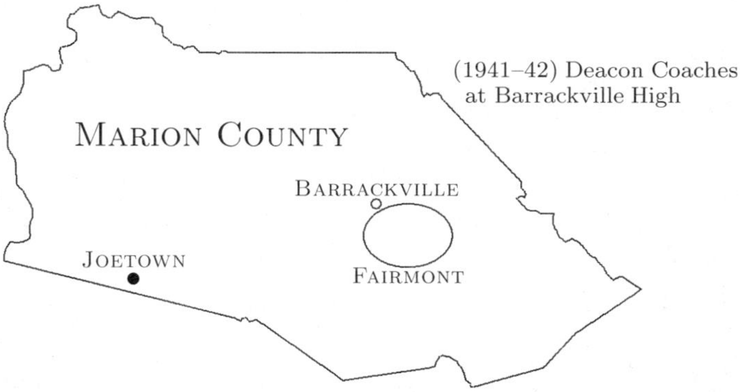

Spring 1941 was his first semester of coaching at the high-school level. And in the summer of 1941, Deacon returned to Columbia University where he completed another 12 hours of graduate studies. Then in the fall of 1941, he rotated back for another year of teaching and coaching at Barrackville.

Deacon near Seneca Rocks in West Virginia (1941)

[9]As part of the offer there was a provision that Deacon had to eventually finish his Masters Degree. So he started to rotate between graduate work at Columbia University in the summer, and teaching and coaching at Barrackville High School during the fall, winter, and spring.

1941–42 Barrackville High School Basketball team
Deacon Duvall Head Coach
Class A State Runnerup[10]

In his first full year (1941-42) at Barrackville Deacon coached a team that was playing for a championship — *Deacon had the basketball team playing in the state finals for the state title.* Deacon's wife Florence attended all of Deacon's games. Deacon remembers Florence as a true coach's wife — as for his high-school coaching days, Florence created two notebooks that contain every article concerning every game that Deacon coached. One of the notebooks was devoted to Deacon's years of coaching at Barrackville, which may still be in housed in the Barrackville Community Center.

[10]FRONT ROW, LEFT-TO-RIGHT: Don Bensey, Asst. Mgr.; John Glance; June Richardson; Ed Janicki; Frank Conaway; Tom Tennant; James Saunders; Howard Floyd, Asst. Mgr.; SECOND ROW: J. Sakie, Asst. Mgr.; Carl Ambrose; Jack Conaway; Coach Deacon Duvall; Bernard Surphin; Bill Garlitz; Jack Weekley, Mgr.; BACK ROW: Fred Wilson; James Martin; Bill Straight; John Charlton; Jr. Dodrill; "Boo" Ice; Jr. Snodderly. STARTING FIVE: F – June Richardson; F – Frank Conaway; C – Ed Janicki; F – Bill Garlitz; G – Tom Tennant; G – John Glance (Ed Janicki became ineligible after seventh game). In the Championship Game, Barrackville lost to Marsh Fork. Final record 5 loses and 21 wins.

While working full time, however, he never lost sight of the sport he was destined to coach, namely, football.

1940s Defensive Football

In the 1940s, while teaching and coaching, and while going to summer school at Columbia University, Deacon still took time to keep up with football at the national level.

He followed the progress of the legendary coach Earl (Red) Blake, who had one of the best college football teams in the nation. As Deacon will tell you, their two running backs, Doc Blanchard and Glenn Davis are remembered to this day. But as great as those two backs were, the key to their total domination was their defense. Deacon views Coach Blake as an innovator and a pioneer. In Deacon's words,

> During Blake's time as a coach, the universally used defensive formation was a 6-2-2-1, i.e., a six-man defensive front, two linebackers, two defensive backs, and a safety. Coach Blake, however, devised a new defensive formation 5-3-2-1, i.e., a five-man front, three linebackers, two defensive halfbacks, and a safety. He included a few defensive stunts where he committed one linebacker to shooting a gap and getting into the opponents backfield. If you are a football fan today, you have seen four-man defensive fronts, and to a lesser degree three-man defensive lines with five linebackers. Up to 1952 and later, West Virginia teams had not progressed very far beyond the six-man defensive fronts.

1942–46 Deacon Serves his Country[11]

During the four-year period 1939–1942 Deacon was very busy: He had graduated from Fairmont State and met Florence (1939), entered Columbia University (1940) for graduate studies in physical education, married Florence (1941), taken his Barrackville Basketball team (1941–42) to the state finals, and had worked for Bethlehem Mines as a block and cement miner's assistant (summer of 1942).[12]

On the world front, 1939–1942 spanned more than half of World War II — it was 1939 when Germany and Soviet Russia signed a non-aggression pact, allowing Germany to invade Poland. Germany's invasion of Poland in 1939 caused England and France to declare war. The United States did not enter World War II until after Japan bombed Pearl Harbor in 1941.

[11] World War II dates from 1939 to 1945.

[12] His summer of 1942 mining experience near Barrackville made him a better teacher and coach because most of his students and players had fathers who worked in the West Virginia coal mines.

Ironically, it would turn out that another 1939 world event would change Deacon's life — Albert Einstein wrote to President Roosevelt in 1939 informing him that nuclear chain reactions could be created and used in bombs.

In December 1942 Deacon's world and world events converge. Uncle Sam called — Deacon was inducted into the armed services (Air Corps). He was about one month short of his 26th birthday when he received his notice.

The war tide was rolling — Germany had captured Denmark and Norway in 1940, and then executed a massive attack on Russia in 1941, the same year that the Japanese killed over 2000 seamen at Pearl Harbor.

Deacon became a First Lieutenant stationed in Laurenburg-Maxton Air Base, North Carolina. Since he had graduate training in physical-education, Uncle Sam used his talents as Convalescent-Orientation Officer.

The build-up continued: In 1943 war contractors issued a directive prohibiting racial discrimination, and President Roosevelt called for a $100 billion military budget. In 1944, Roosevelt was elected for his fourth term as President, and Harry Truman was elected as Vice President.

Even with World-War II ongoing, prior to August 1945 Deacon had not been stationed overseas. But in August of 1945, Deacon was sitting on his duffel bag ready to depart for Japan. *On that very day, however, the Atomic Bomb was dropped, and his orders were canceled.*

1944 Train Trip

In March 1944, Deacon applied and was accepted into the US Air Force Officer Candidate School at Miami Beach, Florida. It was a four-month tour. And after two months, Deacon's wife Florence joined him in Miami Beach. They found a nice apartment and it was a great time for the Duvalls because most folks were eager to do nice things for military families.

While enjoying the beach each day, Florence met wives of other cadets and formed a few friendships.

Deacon successfully completed his four months of schooling, and the day he graduated in June 1944 all cadets boarded trains to various cites where they would be assigned permanent duty. Many of the cadets, Deacon included, were going to Indianapolis, Indiana to receive their orders. Deacon and Florence were traveling with another couple.

The other couple liked to play Hearts, a card game that Deacon never really enjoyed. Deacon had been playing Contract Bridge, but the couple riding with Deacon and Florence had not played Bridge, so the game of the day was Hearts.

Soon after a game of Hearts was underway, however, the train conductor announced that the train would have a 20-minute stop in Macon, Georgia. So deciding to get a newspaper, Deacon got off the train.

When he returned to the boarding station several other trains had arrived, making for a confusing situation. Deacon was alarmed. Then, seeing a train ready to pull out, he jumped onto the moving train. It turned out that he was on the wrong train, but headed in the right direction — the destination was Indianapolis. As his train was leaving the station, Deacon saw Florence through a window, but she did not see him.

The conductor assured Deacon that both trains, the one that Deacon was on and the one that his wife was on, would be pulling into Indianapolis at about the same time.

There were no phones, and no way to contact Florence. And to make the situation worse, Florence had no idea what had happened to her husband and she was carrying no ready cash.

Deacon's train arrived first, and Deacon stood on the deck waiting for Florence for about 20 minutes. Then Florence's train arrived, and as she was leaving her train, she saw Deacon waving his arms. Florence was exceptionally glad to see her husband, telling him, *I believe you did that to keep from playing (the card game) Hearts.*

1946–52 Deacon Assigned to Rivesville

Discharged from the Air Force in May of 1946, but still on reserve duty, Coach Duvall was assigned (from Barrackville) to Rivesville High School.

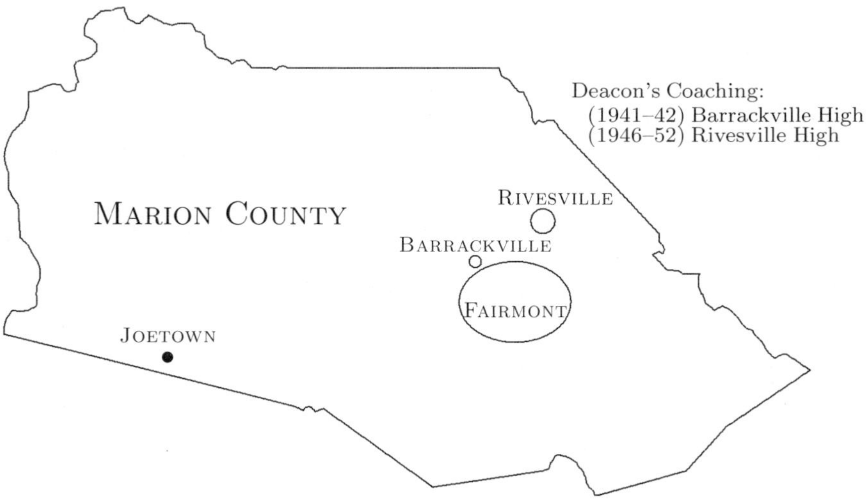

At Rivesville, Coach Duvall was the only coach. His responsibilities included varsity football, varsity basketball, junior-high and 8th-grade basketball and baseball teams. (Surely they could have found something else to keep Deacon busy!)

Deacon's Rivesville football team played against the Farmington-High team when Farmington had a young player who eventually played for both the New York Giants and the Washington Redskins. His name is *Sam Huff.*[13]

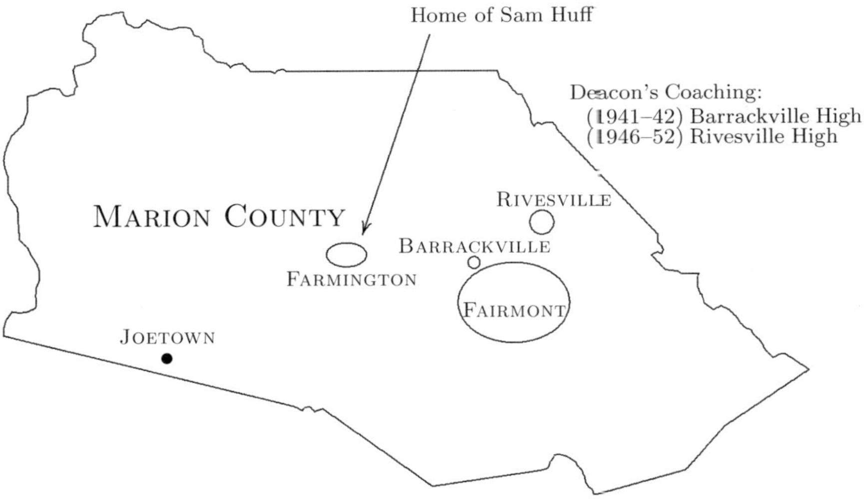

Sam Huff is Robert "Sam" Huff. He grew up in Farmington where he played high-school football. As Chuck Landon, writing in the *Charleston Daily Mail* on July 5, 1999 tells us, Farmington's Sam Huff turned middle linebacker into a glamour position while starring for the New York Giants and the Washington Redskins.

> *As Deacon tells us*: My wife and I were at Farmington attempting to find carpeting for our new home. Across the street from Manchins Carpet Center we heard a strong voice. Someone said, *We are going to get you this fall Coach*!
>
> It was late March and I had not been concentrating on football, but that statement got my attention. I was aware of the fact that Rivesville had seldom, if ever, beaten Farmington in football.
>
> I asked the salesman, *Who made that statement*? The salesman replied, *He is one of Farmington's football players — Robert Huff, but they call him 'Sam.'* The salesman went on to say, *They say he is going to be a good player.*
>
> After that day, I turned my attention to football. And with football six months away, the Rivesville-never-beats-Farmington attitude ignited a burning desire to whip those rascals.
>
> I spent a considerable amount of time thinking about the game, and when fall football practice began, it almost became an obsession — *we must beat Farmington.*
>
> The Farmington game was our last game of the season, and although we had already lost two games, the Farmington game was do or die. So we played the game. It was unbelievable, and it still haunts me.

[13] After his National Football League (NFL) playing days, Sam Huff was inducted into the NFL Hall of Fame.

> Sam was relatively large and quick, making it nearly impossible for our Rivesville players to take him head on. But as a team, we did have some success against Sam — instead of trying to take him head on, the scheme was to block Sam from the side, i.e., use "trap blocks."
>
> At half time, we were ahead by the score of 19-to-7. And had it not been for a major penalty on a questionable trap block, we would have had another chance to score right before half-time — we would have had the ball on Farmington's two-yard line. In addition, we only punted once during the entire game.
>
> We were leading for most of the game. Nevertheless, as the game was nearing an end, Sam picked up a fumble and scored the winning touchdown. That is, we lost 27-to-26.
>
> As always, it is the final score that counts. Sam was right, Farmington beat Rivesville.

God-Given Ability to Lead

Throughout history certain people have shown an innate ability to lead groups of people. Most historians generally study leaders who were involved in major wars, wars that changed civilizations. And while we find these *leaders of men* in all areas of society, it is far easier to come to agreement of exactly who the leaders are when it comes to sports.

One cannot *a priori* (before hand) know who will and who will not be a leader. A leader is usually only recognized after he has been in a position to lead, and then had outstandingly major success. One could rightfully say that the human trait of "leadership" is for the most part one of those elusive characteristics resistant to *a priori* analysis — it can only be truly recognized from an historical viewpoint.

You know it when to see it, but you cannot define it.[14]

Nevertheless, in Coach Duvall's case it was there before our eyes even before he coached his first college-level game in 1952. To be sure, we are not saying that we should have been able to predict his super success as a college coach, but we can say that in fact the indicators of leadership ability were there before 1952.

Early Indicators of Deacon's Ability to Lead

Prior to 1952, most of Deacon's professional experience as a coach was in the context of coaching at the high-school level. So for early indicators of his

[14] For example, we can *historically testify* that Vince Lombardi was a leader because of what he accomplished. But when Vince was only an assistant coach for the New York Giants, the Giants' Management, whose job is that of judging leadership, certainly did not know of Vince's exceptional God-given ability to lead men. I know this because had Management known of his ability, they would have immediately offered Vince the New York Giants Head Football Coach position.

ability to lead, let us focus on his teaching and coaching days at Rivesville, i.e., the days just prior to his first year of college coaching.

In Coach Duvall's case, we have the historical fact that under Deacon's leadership during his first full year of coaching at the high-school level he had his basketball team playing for a State Title.

In addition, we may look back and read three testimonials, the first a 1948 *Senior Class Dedication* of Rivesville High-School students, the second a letter from one of his student-athletes who played for Deacon at both the high school and college levels, and the third a telling poem by one of his high-school colleagues:

First, we have the 1948 *Senior Class Dedication* from Rivesville High-school students. The original is copied below:

WE, the SENIOR CLASS of nineteen hundred and forty-eight, respectfully dedicate this CAMPUS SHADOWS to

Harold "Deacon" Duvall

For his abilities as a TEACHER, COUNSELLOR, and COACH we are truly appreciative.

For his guidance in class and on the athletic field and floor, he merits our respect.

For his natural attributes of kindliness, under-standing and fair play, he deserves his place as a leader of boys.

"And when the great score comes,
To write against your name,
He'll ask not if you won or lost
But how you played the game."

To understand the second testimonial, recall the icon of visual leaders from the movies, namely John Wayne. You may pick almost any of his movies because he always played the role of a leader. Somehow for some reason, there are certain people whom instantly gain our respect as a leader. Call it *charisma*. Call it *a command of one's being*. Call it *a follow-me-men presence*. Whatever you call it, it equates to the "John Wayne effect."

With the John-Wayne effect in mind, let us consider the testimonial of Fred Toothman. Fred was one of Coach Duvall's student-athletes, playing for Deacon both at the high school and college levels. Fred wrote his testimonial (reproduced word-for-word below) in 1994, after he had played football for Deacon at Fairmont State:

Harold S. Duvall

I must write a few words about a man I have always admired and felt privileged to call Coach, Harold S. Duvall.

In the summer of 1946 the sports item read, "H. S. "Deacon" Duvall, named to coach at Rivesville High". My dad exclaimed, "Rivesville has a real coach now. He'll straighten all of them out." I was dumb as a road sign, so I ask my dad what "Deacon" meant. He said. "He's high up in the church, almost a preacher."

School always started the day after Labor Day and the first football game was played on Friday after school started. All of the younger boys, especially me, got as close to the home bench as possible. Coach Duvall didn't like to lose, didn't like mistakes and in no uncertain terms made it known.

When I got home after the game I ask my dad, "Are you sure you gave me the right definition of Deacon?"

Coach Duvall was the Phys. Ed. and health teacher as well as the Football, Basketball, and Baseball coach, at R.H.S.

He taught me "Health" in the 7th grade and I Remember him teaching the 7 basic foods, among other things. Well, Coach Duvall's greatest asset was "influence". He could convince me about anything and everything. Now, at Baxter, we only had three of the basic 7, potatoes, Beans and Bread, So I ate those three foods <u>twice</u> per day and one of them <u>three times</u> that made 7, I thought.

By the time I got to the 8th grade, the coach had me convinced that hitting a player head on in football, was better than "Christmas".

One day, when I was a sophomore, we were scrimmaging, and being a scrub I was a defensive half-back. My cousin, Big Bob Toothman, 6′1″, 195lb full back, came roaming through the line on a cross buck play. Here came Fred, 5′7″, 125lbs. I said to myself, "here comes Christmas" I lowered my head and met Big Bob, head on. Not only did he knock me back 10 yards, he even stepped on me to boot. As I crawled to the side lines I was thinking, "If this is Christmas, what in the hell kind of Santa Claus does Coach Duvall have?"

To say Coach Duvall has had a great influence on my life, is the under statement of my life. He taught me to place kick and would do anything to help me. He snapped the ball, held the ball and would even shag the ball. Sometimes it was almost dark, the teaching paid off as my toe was the difference in 2 high school games. In college, I kicked a field goal against Shepherd College that gave my team a 15–14 win. The year was 1957, and we went on to an undefeated season, winning the W.V.I.A.C. crown.

Coach Duvall taught me many things, but the one I most remember was, "Give it all you got and you'll be surprised at the results."

Coach Duvall is in the WV and N.A.I.A. hall of fame. He's in my hall of fame too.

8-25-94, Fred

The third testimonial is a poem written by Byron Tennant, a colleague of Deacon's when Deacon was teaching and coaching at Rivesville High School. The poem was written on February 15, 1968, a few months after Fairmont State won the National NAIA Football Title:

Dedicated to the Falcon Football Team of 1967

If you can have your boys in top condition
And mentally alert all through the day
If you can bet your all on one maneuver
And then come through with one big winning play
If you can trade possession for position
Then, all unmindful of the cynics roar,
Take the break that comes from your decision
Get the ball, move down the field, and score

If you can keep your faith in all your players
And they, in turn, have confidence in you
If you can meet with failure and disaster
And yet not gripe too much nor get too blue
If you can work with everything that's in you
But still remember football's partly fun
So have some laughs and get some relaxation
It might pay off before the season's done

If you can win but not be spoiled by winning
Take all the trophies and honors of last fall
Yet keep your poise, count modesty a virtue
Try not to think too big nor stand too tall
If you can teach your boys to block and tackle
Full sixty minutes out of every fray
And play the kind of vicious, hard-nosed football
Your coaches used to get from you each day

If you can dream yet not make dreams your master
But by hardwork make all your dreams come true
If you can fight when every nerve and sinew
Is crying out and everything seems gone
But still hold on when there is nothing in you
Except the will which says to you hold on
If you can plan, give every plan a reason
And every reason backed by all your will
Then you can have another perfect season
and another national championship on the hill

1952 and Deacon is Ready to Move Up

With one and one-half years of coaching at Barrackville, and six full years at Rivesville, Deacon was ready to move up to college-level coaching. Both Barrackville and Rivesville were relatively small schools when compared to the schools that they regularly competed against. At Rivesville, the second smallest high school in a county of eight, Deacon's teams were mostly competing against larger schools. His experience as a coach at these small high schools taught him that there was a need to develop strategies so that smaller boys could compete with larger boys — a 130-pound boy couldn't be expected to manhandle a 170-pounder head on. Deacon found a solution in his study of the *Notre Dame* T.

The solution was the use of a *trap block*, a block from the side and not head on. A trap block allows his 130-pound blocker to neutralize the 170-pound tackler's size and charge. The chance of success of a trap block increases in direct proportion to the speed of the tackler's charge.

At the high-school level, Coach Duvall had substantial experience and success with the Notre Dame T. Under the "T" system over two seasons, the 1950 and 1951 seasons, his high-school teams had ten wins, five losses, and one tie.

In summary of this Postscript, it is now 1952 and Deacon moves up to Fairmont State.

APPENDIX

Local Sports Icons

On the personal side, to know Coach Duvall is to know of his feelings about being a native of Marion County, West Virginia. One aspect of his pride in West Virginia in general and in Marion County in particular is perhaps best illustrated by one of his questions, namely, *How could such a relatively small population living in such a relatively small area produce more than a century of sports icons*? By *sports icons* he means athletes and coaches who went on to exceptional greatness at the national and international levels.[1]

But let us focus on the background for Deacon's question. This Appendix documents the fact that for more than a century, Marion County and the surrounding areas have produced a continuing and truly-exceptional supply of successful sports icons. For Deacon, it is their character, their work ethic, their determination to succeed, and their belief systems that are important. Such characteristics have served to shape many of his thoughts and values.[2]

FIELDING (HURRY-UP) YOST (1871–1946)

Fielding (Hurry-Up) Yost was born in Fairview, located in Marion County, West Virginia. (See the map on the following page.) His grandson Fielding Yost III attended Fairmont State and was a regular on the basketball team. Coach Duvall believes that *it is most likely that Fielding's outstanding success was a motivating factor in Cam Henderson's decision to become a coach.*

Fielding coached at Nebraska in 1898, with a winning percentage of 72.7, at Kansas in 1899 where he went undefeated, and at San José State in 1900 with a winning percentage of 50. Fielding served as Head Football Coach for the Michigan Wolverines football team from 1901 through 1923, and again in 1925 and 1926 with a winning percentage of 83.3. At Michigan, from 1901–05, Yost's football teams were undefeated in 56 straight games, outscoring Michigan's opponents 2,821 to 42. Those teams were called the

[1]When Deacon was a young boy, in the 1920s and 30s, there was necessarily an emphasis on *local sports icons* because it was the 1920s when radio broadcasts were just starting to expand, and it wasn't until the 1950s that television became commonplace. Nevertheless, even today, as the National Football League programming illustrates, people prefer their local teams, their local coaches, and their local athletes.

[2]There is no pretense of presenting complete histories of the people mentioned in this appendix. The goal here is to document a few facts about a few local sports icons who had an impact on Coach Duvall's thoughts and values.

"point-a-minute" squads. His teams won six National Championships and ten Big Ten titles.

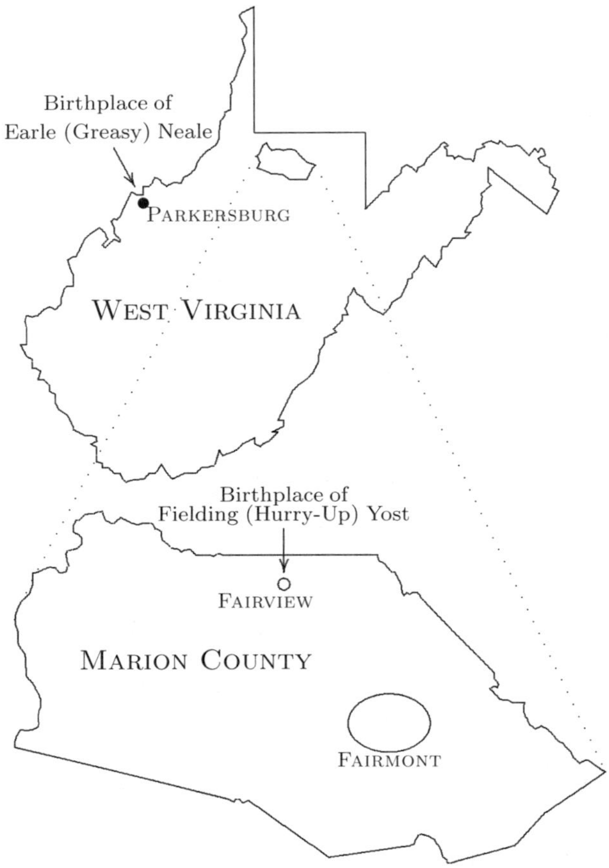

Birthplaces of Fielding (Hurry-Up) Yost and Earle (Greasy) Neale.

EARLE (GREASY) NEALE (1891–1973)

Earle (Greasy) Neale was born in Parkersburg, West Virginia. Parkersburg is located near the Ohio River less than 100 miles west of Fairmont. He is a member of both the College Football Hall of Fame and the Pro Football (NFL) Hall of Fame. As Head Coach of the Philadelphia Eagles (1941–1950), the Eagles won two NFL titles (1948 and 1949).

It was 2004 when Andy Reid, the current Eagles Head Coach, hit 66 career wins. And at 66 wins, Reid is the only Eagles coach who managed to tie Earl (Greasy) Neale as the all-time winningest coach in Eagles history.

Before he coached the Eagles, Neale starred as an end on Jim Thorpe's pre World War I Canton Bulldogs.

Neale was also a successful college coach, leading Washington and Jefferson College to the 1922 Rose Bowl. He was Head Football Coach at both the

University of Virginia (1923–28) and West Virginia University (1931–33).

Neale was also an outfielder in Major League Baseball (1916–1924), spending all but 22 games of his career with the Cincinnati Reds. He finished in the top 10 in stolen bases in the National League four times.

Frank Gatski (1919–2005)

Like Sam Huff, Frank Gatski was born in Farmington, West Virginia. Frank's older brother and young Harold Duvall were competitors in high-school basketball — Frank's brother played for Farmington when Deacon played for Fairmont West.

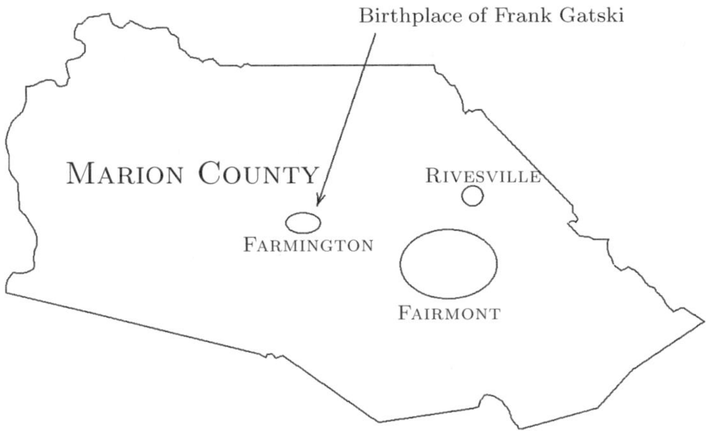

Frank Gatski's birthplace, Farmington, West Virginia.

Frank Gatski (right) and Deacon share a moment.

Frank attended Marshall and Auburn Universities where he played as a center and linebacker. He then played center for the Cleveland Browns (1946–56) and the Detroit Lions (1957). In those twelve seasons, Gatski's teams played for the league title 11 times. Moreover, Frank was inducted into the National Football League (NFL) Hall of Fame in 1985 with a class that included Joe Namath and Roger Staubach.

Coach Duvall grew to admire and respect Frank. When Deacon was football coach (1946–52) at Rivesville High, Frank would at times assist Deacon by coaching some of the Rivesville football players, especially the centers. In the picture above, Frank and Deacon were attending a banquet honoring Frank's accomplishments as a Marion-County athlete.

Marshall University retired Gatski's number "72" on October 15, 2005, the first Marshall football player to be so honored. On November 18, 2006 the East End Bridge was renamed the *Frank Gatski Memorial Bridge.*

Rich Rodriguez (1963–)

Rich Rodriguez was born on May 24, 1963 in Grant Town, West Virginia. He is currently the Head Football Coach at West Virginia University (WVU).

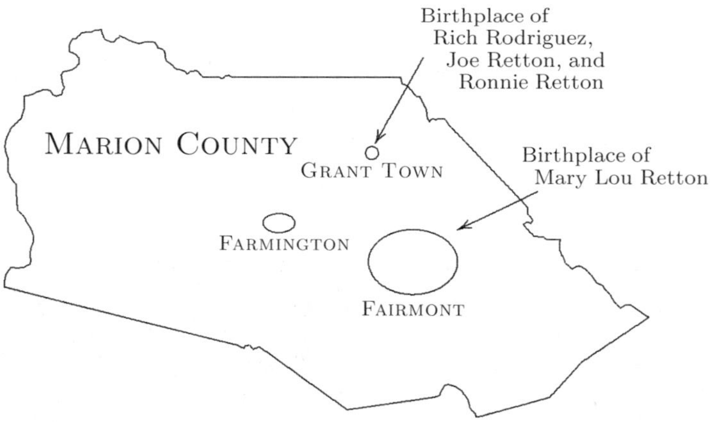

Coach Rod graduated from North Marion High School in 1981, where he played four sports and made All State in both football and basketball. After his high-school days, he went to WVU as a student, where he played WVU football as a "walk-on" and later earned a scholarship. His first coaching positions were at WVIAC schools — first Salem College, and later 1990–1996 Glenville State. While at Glenville, his teams won three consecutive WVIAC championships and played in the 1993 NAIA National Championship Game. He was WVIAC Coach of the year in 1993 and 1994, NAIA Coach of the Year in 1993, and West Virginia State College Coach of the Year in 1993.

After Glenville, Rodriguez served as assistant coach, offensive coordinator, and quarterback coach under Tommy Bowden, who was Head Coach at

Tulane. And when Bowden was hired as head coach at Clemson, Rodriguez joined his staff.

Rodriguez is considered one of the greatest coaches in West Virginia history — he coached WVU to its first back-to-back top ten NCAA Division I finishes, four consecutive Bowl appearances, WVU's first BCS Bowl win, three Big East Championships, and the list goes on.

Coach Rod is considered a pioneer for creating the so-called *Spread-Option Offense*, which he introduced at Glenville State and currently employs at WVU.

As for Deacon's view of Coach Rod's "spread-option offense," let us have Deacon tell his story:

> I first saw Coach Rod's spread-option offense when Rodriguez was coaching at Glenville State. He was having sensational success and was reputed to have developed a new offensive system that was taking the WVIAC by storm. Having watched the development of several offensive systems over the years, including the Split-T, Inside and Outside Belly, and West Coach offenses, I was anxious to see Coach Rod's new offense.
>
> To my surprise, the players lined up in the Shotgun Formation. I immediately recalled my Fairmont State playing days in late 1930s — our offensive scheme also had the players line up in the Shotgun Formation. In particular, during my senior year 1937, we started the season trying to develop a running game with the Single Wing, but we were unsuccessful. So we eased into the Double Wing, but again our running game was unsuccessful. Eventually we went to what we called the *Short Punt* Formation. In layman's terms, because we could not run the football we simply lined up with the quarterback five-yards deep, trying to complete passes to the wing backs.
>
> Because of my experience from the 1930s with the short-punt formation (see page 119) — today's Shot Gun — I just assumed that Coach Rod was in trouble and was using the Shot Gun as a last resort. In the old days, we didn't think you could run from the Shot Gun formation because we did not pull linemen to lead the ball carrier. In contrast, to lead the ball carrier the single-wing schemes of the 1930s had either both guards pulling or a guard and tackle pulling.
>
> It became clear that Coach Rodriguez *had developed a running game from the Shot Gun Formation.* He had done his homework, and his innovative rendition of the old Short Punt was a modern and respected mode of attack — many coaches today have borrowed from his ideas.

And Deacon is correct, many have borrowed from Rich Rodriguez's ideas. Certainly the University of Alabama has followed Rod's spread-option offense — one of the 2007 national sports stories told how Coach Rodriguez was offered several million dollars to leave West Virginia University to become Head Football Coach at the University of Alabama. As that story played out, however, Coach Rodriguez decided to stay in his home state of West Virginia, continuing to coach at WVU. And for the rest of the story, after Coach Rodriguez declined the offer, the University of Alabama hired *another Marion County native — Nick Saban.* (See FINDING SOLUTIONS AT THE NAVAL ACADEMY in Chapter 4.)

MARY LOU RETTON (1968–)[3]

Mary Lou Retton was born in 1968 in Fairmont, West Virginia (see map in previous section). Mary Lou was the first female gymnast outside of Eastern Europe to win the Olympic All-Around Title. She was inspired by the success of Nadia Comăneci, and so she started training in gymnastics in Fairmont, where she was coached by Gary Rafaloski. She then moved to Houston, Texas, where she trained under the Béla and Marta Károlyi, who had mentored Nadia Comăneci. For her 1984 Olympic Gold Medal performance, Sports Illustrated magazine named her *Sportswoman of the Year.* She appeared on a Wheaties box, and became the cereal's first official spokeswoman. Her infectious smile and personality was captured in a 1984 (now famous) photo that featured her and then President Ronald Reagan standing in front of the 1984 United States Olympic Team.

Mary Lou Retton was elected into the National Italian American Sports Hall of Fame in 1992. And in 1997 she was inducted into the International gymnastics Hall of Fame.

JOE RETTON (1931–)

Like Rich Rodriguez, Joe Retton was born in Grant Town, West Virginia (see map in Section RICH RODRIGUEZ.) Joe Retton, who is Mary Lou Retton's cousin, is often referred to as a *legendary basketball coach.* For good reasons, Deacon rates Joe among the greatest basketball coaches of all time. Although he never had the opportunity to coach at the NCAA Division I level, he did, however, compile an amazing record.

At the smallest high school in Marion county, Coach Retton had 147 wins and 19 losses. That is an 88.55 percent winning record! He also had a perfect 27 wins in his 1961 undefeated season at Barrackville High School.

At Fairmont State, he was named WVIAC and NAIA *District* 28 *Coach of the Year* six times. He was also named NAIA *Coach of the Year* in 1969

[3] Mary Lou's father was *Ronnie Retton*, who played guard and was captain of the WVU 1959 NCAA runner-up basketball team which featured the NBA great Jerry West. Ronnie was also an All-Conference baseball selection and a short stop who batted .270 over his first four of six seasons in the Yankee's Farm System.

and 1976; and in 1975–76, he was named *Associated Press Small College Coach of the Year.*

His teams made 12 NAIA Tournament appearances — four times in the Final Four with the 1967–68 squad in the finals. His teams also appeared in 12 WVIAC Championships.

Coach Retton had 18 straight seasons of 20 or more victories. The 1975–76 team was ranked first in the Final Associated Press Small College Basketball Poll. Two of his teams had undefeated regular seasons, namely, his 1970–71 and 1975–76 teams. Joe Retton was inducted into the NAIA Coaches Hall of Fame; the West Virginia Sports Hall of Fame, and the Fairmont State Hall of Fame. In fact, his career record was 478–95 (83.4%) — *Retton was the 'winningest' collegiate coach by percentage in the nation.*

Samuel (toothpick) Jones (1925–1971)

Although Sam (Toothpick) Jones was born in Stewartsville, Ohio, he grew up in Nick Saban's Monongah, West Virginia. Unlike Nick, however, Sam Jones was a professional baseball player. Surprisingly, Sam did not try out for his high-school baseball team; and as a result, he was not known locally for his great pitching ability, i.e., not until he played in the Majors.

It was after he was inducted into the Army in World War II that his exceptional pitching ability was noticed. Toothpick was playing service baseball, and his fellow solders recognized Sam's unusual and natural talent. Later a professional baseball scout took notice — Sam was signed by the Cleveland Indians as an amateur free agent in 1950, and his debut came on September 22, 1951. He played his final game on October 3, 1964.

The Marion county locals were quite surprised by Sam Jones abilities, who they analyzed as someone who was a bit lazy and didn't want to do much of anything. They even thought that there must be another Sam Jones in this community; but it was their Sam, and his success was a shock.

Sam pitched for Cleveland, the Chicago Cubs, Saint Louis, San Francisco, Detroit, and Baltimore. His claim to fame, however, came as the result of a *no hit, no run* game he pitched for the San Francisco Giants against the Pittsburgh Pirates. From Deacon's view, Sam is an example of thousands of Americans who have unbelievable talent, but for whatever reason they may never use or reveal their great abilities.

And There are Others ...

There were other icons. One can only guess how many young boys were influenced by sports icons like Cam Henderson, who was born in Joetown, West Virginia (see The Cam Henderson Connection in the Editor's Introduction).

For an example consider *Clare Bee.* Clare was raised in Taylor County, West Virginia, which is right next door to Marion County. He was a coach at Grafton, which is in Taylor County. Clare also played basketball *in the game where Cam Henderson introduced the Zone Defense.*[4]

Clare Bee went on to coach basketball at Long Island University in New York, where he had a 43 consecutive-game win streak.[5]

Up to that time, 43 was the college record for consecutive wins. Bee's Long Island Blackbirds were undefeated in 1935 and 1939, and won the NIT when it superseded the NCAA.

Also consider *Joe Stydahar.* Arguably, Joe may have been the finest tackle Coach George Halas of the Chicago Bears ever had. Well you guessed it! Joe grew up near Marion County — in Harrison County, West Virginia, just eight miles from Cam's birthplace Joetown. Joe played college football at West Virginia University and after his professional career, he was inducted into the NFL Football Hall of Fame.

Also consider *Cliff "the Gip" Battles.* Cliff was a 6′ 1″ 190-pound tailback from West Virginia Wesleyan.[6]

George Preston Marshall (owner of the newly formed Boston Braves, known today as the Washington Redskins) saw Battles play in a 1931 game against Georgetown. And in 1932 Battles was offered contracts from the New York Giants and the Portsmouth Spartans. But Battles chose the Boston Braves because they were the only team to send someone to personally see him in West Virginia.

In his first year, the Gip won the NFL rushing title — he ran for more yards than Red Grange, Bronko Nagurski, etc. And in 1937, Battles, a 201-pound fullback, together with "Slingin" Sammy Baugh led the Washington Redskins to their first NFL Championship. Both Battles and Baugh are members of the NFL Hall of Fame.

Local Military Icon George Roberts

So far we have only considered local sports icons whose character, whose work ethic, whose determination to succeed, and whose belief systems made them exceptionally successful. Such characteristics are not, however, limited to athletes and coaches — the US Military contains many men with such characteristics, and one such local military icon is *George "Spanky" Roberts.*

---

[4]In addition to the offset paragraph (page 116) in The Cam Henderson Connection section in the Editor's Postscript, there is a substantial historical account of the The Birth of the Zone in Sam Clagg's book, *The Cam Henderson Story, His Life and Times.*

[5]See page 80 in Sam Clagg's book, *The Cam Henderson Story, His Life and Times,* where it is noted that "*As a college coach, ...*" Bee "*dropped only a dozen games in more than* 120 *played ....*"

[6]West Virginia Wesleyan is about 40 miles south of Fairmont.

Following George's graduation from Fairmont's old Dunbar High School, he went on to establish himself as the first black commander in World War II. He was among the first of those accepted into the famed *Tuskegee Airmen* program, and he was among its first five graduates. He rose to the rank of Colonel and was awarded command of the 99th Fighter Squadron — the first all-black squadron in the US Air Force in World War II. He flew 103 combat missions.

And the List Goes On ...

There was also *Horace Lowe*, who was born in Fairview, West Virginia. He played football at West Virginia University, and later became the football and basketball coach, and then Athletic Director at Potomac State College in Keyser, West Virginia. And speaking of Athletic Directors, Fairmont State's *Squibb Wilson* was also a Fairview native.

And if we were to start adopting those sports icons of national fame who spent a substantial part of their careers in West Virginia, we would have to include the winningest Coach in Division I NCAA history *Bobby Bowden*, former well-known Head Football Coach at West Virginia University.

In summary, as Deacon would say, *Given the relatively small population living in such a relatively small area surrounding Marion County, and given the exceptional national and international success of the local sports icons that the area has produced over the last century, Marion County must qualify for the title "Capital of Sports Icons."*

INDEX